CAMBRIDGE

Shakespeare

All's Well That Ends Well

Edited by Elizabeth Huddlestone and Sheila Innes

Series Editor: Rex Gibson
Director, Shakespeare and Schools Project

CAMBRIDGE
UNIVERSITY PRESS

Published by the Press Syndicate of the University of Cambridge
The Pitt Building, Trumpington Street, Cambridge CB2 1RP
40 West 20th Street, New York, NY 10011-4211, USA
10 Stamford Road, Oakleigh, Melbourne 3166, Australia

First published 1993

Printed in Great Britain at the University Press, Cambridge

A catalogue record for this book is available from the British Library

Library of Congress cataloguing in publication data applied for

ISBN 0 521 44583 3 paperback

Designed by Richard Morris, Stonesfield Design
Picture research by Callie Kendall

Thanks are due to the following for permission to reproduce photographs:

p. 8, by permission of The British Library, London; pp. 16, 54, 74, 94, 187*c*, The Shakespeare Centre Library, Stratford-upon-Avon; pp. 20*t*, 79*b*, 118, 187*t*, The Shakespeare Centre Library, Stratford-upon-Avon: Joe Cocks Studio Collection; pp. 20*bl*, 152, 170, © BBC; pp. 20*br*, 104*bl*, by permission of the Stamford Shakespeare Company; pp. 26, 80, 100, 104*tl*, Donald Cooper © Photostage; pp. 50, 104*tr*, 130, Angus McBean; p. 79*t*, Angus McBean/ Harvard Theatre Collection; pp. 136, 1959 Shakespeare Memorial Theatre production: impression by Neil Harvey; p. 142, Ivan Kyncl; p. 146, Stuart Morris; p. 147*l*, Devonshire Collection, Chatsworth. Reproduced by permission of the Chatsworth Settlement Trustees; p. 147*r*, Mary Evans Picture Library; p. 148, by permission of the Board of Trustees of the Victoria & Albert Museum; p. 187*b*, The Shakespeare Centre Library, Stratford-upon-Avon: Tom Holte Theatre Photographic Collection.

GO

Contents

Cambridge School Shakespeare

This edition of *All's Well That Ends Well* is part of the *Cambridge School Shakespeare* series. Like every other play in the series, it has been specially prepared to help all students in schools and colleges.

This *All's Well That Ends Well* aims to be different from other editions of the play. It invites you to bring the play to life in your classroom, hall or drama studio through enjoyable activities that will increase your understanding. Actors have created their different interpretations of the play over the centuries. Similarly, you are encouraged to make up your own mind about *All's Well That Ends Well*, rather than having someone else's interpretation handed down to you.

Cambridge School Shakespeare does not offer you a cut-down or simplified version of the play. This is Shakespeare's language, filled with imaginative possibilities. You will find on every left-hand page: a summary of the action, an explanation of unfamiliar words, a choice of activities on Shakespeare's language, characters and stories.

Between each act and in the pages at the end of the play, you will find notes, illustrations and activities. These will help to increase your understanding of the whole play.

There are a large number of activities to give you the widest choice to suit your own particular needs. Please don't think you have to do every one. Choose the activities that will help you most.

This edition will be of value to you whether you are studying for an examination, reading for pleasure, or thinking of putting on the play to entertain others. You can work on the activities on your own or in groups. Many of the activities suggest a particular group size, but don't be afraid to make up larger or smaller groups to suit your own purposes.

Although you are invited to treat *All's Well That Ends Well* as a play, you don't need special dramatic or theatrical skills to do the activities. By choosing your activities, and by exploring and experimenting, you can make your own interpretations of Shakespeare's language, characters and stories. Whatever you do, remember that Shakespeare wrote his plays to be acted, watched and enjoyed.

Rex Gibson

This edition of *All's Well That Ends Well* uses the text of the play established by Russell Fraser in *The New Cambridge Shakespeare*.

List of characters

Rossillion

COUNTESS OF ROSSILLION
BERTRAM Count of Rossillion (her son)
HELENA DE NARBON a gentlewoman in the Countess's household
LAVATCH a clown, servant to the Countess
PAROLLES a friend of Bertram
RINALDO steward to the Countess
A PAGE

Paris

KING OF FRANCE
LAFEW an old Lord
FIRST LORD Dumaine ⎱
SECOND LORD Dumaine ⎰ lords in the service of the King
Other young lords, Servants

Florence

DUKE OF FLORENCE
WIDOW CAPILET
DIANA her daughter
MARIANA ⎱
VIOLENTA ⎰ neighbours and friends of the Widow
Citizens, Soldiers, Messenger

Marseilles

A GENTLE ASTRINGER a gentleman falconer

The action of the play takes place in Rossillion, Paris, Florence and
Marseilles

The Countess of Rossillion says farewell to her son. He has been commanded to attend the court of the King of France, who is fatally ill. No doctor can cure him.

1 Sorting out the information (in groups of three)

These first lines give a great deal of information. Read them through two or three times. Talk together about what you discover about the characters. Present your information to the rest of the class as a short news report. You could begin: 'Today the young Count of Rossillion took leave of his mother, the Dowager Countess, to go to court . . .'.

2 Declaring the theme?

Shakespeare often introduces at least one of the themes of a play in the first line of the script. The Countess uses the word 'delivering' to mean that she is sending Bertram away from her, but it is used more often to mean 'giving birth'. From line 1, what do you think could be a theme of the play?

3 His majesty the King (in pairs)

Lafew's lines 5–8 suggest that the King is everything to everybody. Make a list of the words which you feel indicate the King's qualities. Compare your list with your partner's.

4 Persecuting time with hope (in groups of three or four)

Present two tableaux (still pictures) of lines 10–12 to show the contrast between the two stages of the King's quest for a cure.

5 Honesty

'Honesty' (honour) is one of the major themes of the play. In lines 14–15 the Countess suggests that, if the doctor's skill as a physician had been as great as his integrity, he would have defeated death.

---

in ward under the king's protection
wanted was lacking
amendment recovery

practices medical treatments
passage word, reference to the past
honesty honour

All's Well That Ends Well

ACT I SCENE I
The Palace of Rossillion

Enter BERTRAM, *the* COUNTESS OF ROSSILLION, LORD LAFEW *and* HELENA, *all in black*

COUNTESS In delivering my son from me, I bury a second husband.

BERTRAM And I in going, madam, weep o'er my father's death anew; but I must attend his majesty's command, to whom I am now in ward, evermore in subjection.

LAFEW You shall find of the king a husband, madam; you, sir, a father. 5
He that so generally is at all times good must of necessity hold his virtue to you, whose worthiness would stir it up where it wanted, rather than lack it where there is such abundance.

COUNTESS What hope is there of his majesty's amendment?

LAFEW He hath abandoned his physicians, madam, under whose 10
practices he hath persecuted time with hope, and finds no other advantage in the process but only the losing of hope by time.

COUNTESS This young gentlewoman had a father – O, that 'had', how sad a passage 'tis – whose skill was almost as great as his honesty; had it stretched so far, would have made nature immortal, and death 15
should have play for lack of work. Would for the king's sake he were living! I think it would be the death of the king's disease.

LAFEW How called you the man you speak of, madam?

COUNTESS He was famous, sir, in his profession, and it was his great right to be so – Gerard de Narbon. 20

*The Countess and Lafew discuss the King's illness, and praise Helena for
her virtue. The Countess gives parting advice to her son, Bertram.*

---

1 Helena's virtues (in pairs)

Read through the Countess's description of Helena (lines 30–5)
twice, taking turns to read a sentence each. Notice how the Countess
stresses Helena's virtue and honour. How do you think Helena feels
as she listens to this?

2 Advice to a young person about to leave home

The Countess is not the only parent to offer advice in a play by
Shakespeare. Here, from *Hamlet*, is some of the advice Polonius
offers to his son, Laertes.

> Those friends thou hast, and their adoption tried,
> Grapple them to thy soul with hoops of steel;
> But do not dull thy palm with entertainment
> Of each new-hatched, unfledged courage. Beware
> Of entrance to a quarrel; but being in,
> Bear't that the opposed may beware of thee . . .
> Costly thy habit as thy purse can buy,
> But not expressed in fancy; rich, not gaudy; . . .
> Neither a borrower nor a lender be;
> For loan oft loses both itself and friend,
> And borrowing dulls the edge of husbandry.
> This above all – to thine own self be true,
> And it must follow, as the night the day,
> Thou canst not then be false to any man.

Compare both pieces of parental advice. Then write your
own advice to a modern young person about to leave home.

---

languishes of is afflicted by	**holy wishes** blessing
fistula painful abcess or ulcer	**blood** inherited qualities
derives inherits	**Contend for empire** struggle for
brine salt water (tears)	dominance
season preserve	**able for** better than
affect pretend, imitate	**checked** criticised
mortal deadly	**unseasoned** inexperienced

LAFEW He was excellent indeed, madam. The king very lately spoke
of him admiringly and mourningly. He was skilful enough to have
lived still, if knowledge could be set up against mortality.

BERTRAM What is it, my good lord, the king languishes of?

LAFEW A fistula, my lord.   25

BERTRAM I heard not of it before.

LAFEW I would it were not notorious. Was this gentlewoman the
daughter of Gerard de Narbon?

COUNTESS His sole child, my lord, and bequeathed to my overlooking.
I have those hopes of her good that her education promises. Her   30
dispositions she inherits, which makes fair gifts fairer; for where
an unclean mind carries virtuous qualities, their commendations go
with pity – they are virtues and traitors too. In her they are the
better for their simpleness. She derives her honesty and achieves
her goodness.   35

LAFEW Your commendations, madam, get from her tears.

COUNTESS 'Tis the best brine a maiden can season her praise in. The
remembrance of her father never approaches her heart but the
tyranny of her sorrows takes all livelihood from her cheek. No more
of this, Helena. Go to, no more, lest it be rather thought you affect   40
a sorrow than to have.

HELENA I do affect a sorrow indeed, but I have it too.

LAFEW Moderate lamentation is the right of the dead; excessive grief
the enemy to the living.

COUNTESS If the living be enemy to the grief, the excess makes it soon   45
mortal.

BERTRAM Madam, I desire your holy wishes.

LAFEW How understand we that?

COUNTESS Be thou blest, Bertram, and succeed thy father
    In manners as in shape. Thy blood and virtue   50
    Contend for empire in thee, and thy goodness
    Share with thy birthright. Love all, trust a few,
    Do wrong to none. Be able for thine enemy
    Rather in power than use, and keep thy friend
    Under thy own life's key. Be checked for silence,   55
    But never taxed for speech. What heaven more will,
    That thee may furnish, and my prayers pluck down,
    Fall on thy head. – Farewell, my lord.
    'Tis an unseasoned courtier; good my lord,
    Advise him.

Left alone, Helena speaks of her secret love for Bertram and the impossibility of her marrying him. Bertram's friend, Parolles, comes in, and Helena comments on his character.

---

1 'That I should love a bright particular star' (in pairs)

a Facing one another, speak Helena's lines 67–86 reading one *line* each alternately. Read them through again, this time speaking one *sentence* alternately. Talk together about the different tone given by each way of reading.

b Choose two sentences each which you feel sum up Helena's feelings, and talk about your choices. Share your choice of sentences with the rest of the class.

c Helena uses the image of a star to demonstrate how far above her Bertram is. Identify the other images she uses to suggest how impossible it is for them to marry. She feels that she could no more marry Bertram than touch a star; her comfort must be in being able to see him. What does this suggest to you about the relationships between social classes in this society?

2 His hawking eye . . .

Who would you cast as Bertram, using Helena's description of him? For example, think of stage, film or television actors.

3 I love him for his sake

Helena is critical of Parolles, yet she says that she loves him just because he is a friend of Bertram's. In Jane Austen's novel *Emma*, Harriet keeps a plaster just because it had once been on Mr Elton's finger. Can you imagine keeping something or loving someone just because of their connection with the person you love?

---

forgèd made
Be comfortable comfort
credit reputation
collateral reflected
in his sphere by physical contact
hind female deer
table notebook

capable both (1) susceptible (her heart), and (2) easy to draw on (her notebook)
trick facial expression
take place are considered superior
waiting on attending on

LAFEW	He cannot want the best	60

That shall attend his love.

COUNTESS   Heaven bless him!

Farewell, Bertram.   [*Exit*]

BERTRAM   The best wishes that can

Be forgèd in your thoughts be servants to you.

[*To Helena*] Be comfortable to my mother, your mistress,

And make much of her.

LAFEW   Farewell, pretty lady.   65

You must hold the credit of your father.

[*Exeunt Bertram and Lafew*]

HELENA O, were that all! I think not on my father,

And these great tears grace his remembrance more

Than those I shed for him. What was he like?

I have forgot him. My imagination   70

Carries no favour in't but Bertram's.

I am undone! There is no living, none,

If Bertram be away. 'Twere all one

That I should love a bright particular star

And think to wed it, he is so above me.   75

In his bright radiance and collateral light

Must I be comforted, not in his sphere.

Th'ambition in my love thus plagues itself.

The hind that would be mated by the lion

Must die for love. 'Twas pretty, though a plague,   80

To see him every hour; to sit and draw

His archèd brows, his hawking eye, his curls,

In our heart's table – heart too capable

Of every line and trick of his sweet favour.

But now he's gone, and my idolatrous fancy   85

Must sanctify his relics. Who comes here?

Enter PAROLLES

One that goes with him. I love him for his sake;

And yet I know him a notorious liar,

Think him a great way fool, solely a coward.

Yet these fixed evils sit so fit in him   90

That they take place when virtue's steely bones

Looks bleak i'th'cold wind. Withal, full oft we see

Cold wisdom waiting on superfluous folly.

Parolles and Helena discuss the merits of virginity. Parolles compares it to a city under siege, then argues that it is against nature to preserve virginity.

1 Is man 'enemy to virginity'? (in pairs)

- List the types of imagery used by Helena and Parolles in talking about the losing of virginity (lines 100–39), for example warfare. How apt do you think they are?
- Why do you think Helena joins in this bawdy conversation?
- Identify Parolles' arguments in favour of losing virginity. Devise and present an argument to counter each of Parolles' reasons, putting the case against losing virginity.

'You lose your city.' A medieval town under siege. A siege had fairly strict conventions which made it sound almost like a game. The reality was much more brutal. Parolles' metaphor is of virginity besieged by man.

'Save you God save you (a greeting)
barricado defend
setting down before besieging, attacking
undermine . . . up lay explosives under (also, make you pregnant)
breach gap in defences

politic sensible
got conceived
infallible certain
paring last tiny bit
inhibited forbidden
canon law of the Church
principal stake money

8

PAROLLES 'Save you, fair queen!

HELENA And you, monarch!   95

PAROLLES No.

HELENA And no.

PAROLLES Are you meditating on virginity?

HELENA Ay. You have some stain of soldier in you: let me ask you a
question. Man is enemy to virginity; how may we barricado it   100
against him?

PAROLLES Keep him out.

HELENA But he assails, and our virginity, though valiant, in the defence
yet is weak. Unfold to us some warlike resistance.

PAROLLES There is none. Man, setting down before you, will undermine   105
you and blow you up.

HELENA Bless our poor virginity from underminers and blowers-up! Is
there no military policy how virgins might blow up men?

PAROLLES Virginity being blown down, man will quicklier be blown
up. Marry, in blowing him down again, with the breach yourselves   110
made, you lose your city. It is not politic in the commonwealth of
nature to preserve virginity. Loss of virginity is rational increase,
and there was never virgin got till virginity was first lost. That you
were made of, is metal to make virgins. Virginity by being once lost
may be ten times found; by being ever kept it is ever lost. 'Tis too   115
cold a companion. Away with't!

HELENA I will stand for't a little, though therefore I die a virgin.

PAROLLES There's little can be said in't; 'tis against the rule of nature.
To speak on the part of virginity is to accuse your mothers, which
is most infallible disobedience. He that hangs himself is a virgin: 120
virginity murders itself, and should be buried in highways out of
all sanctified limit, as a desperate offendress against nature. Virginity
breeds mites, much like a cheese; consumes itself to the very paring,
and so dies with feeding his own stomach. Besides, virginity is
peevish, proud, idle, made of self-love, which is the most inhibited   125
sin in the canon. Keep it not; you cannot choose but lose by't. Out
with't! Within ten year it will make itself two, which is a goodly
increase, and the principal itself not much the worse. Away with't!

HELENA How might one do, sir, to lose it to her own liking?

Parolles urges losing virginity at a young age, before it becomes stale. Helena lists the many qualities a virgin will bring to Bertram as his future wife. Parolles claims that he was born to be a soldier.

1 'There shall your master have a thousand loves' (in pairs)

a Talk together about how Helena changes the tone of the conversation at line 141.

b As one of you slowly reads the twelve 'loves' in lines 142–5, the other makes a gesture and expression to suit each one.

c Do you think Helena is talking about herself in lines 141–50, or listing the conventional images of women in courtly love poetry (see page 34)?

2 Helena's confusion

Helena's confused feelings about Bertram are reflected in her language, which contradicts itself ('humble ambition, proud humility'). This pairing of an adjective with a contradictory noun is called an oxymoron (from two Greek words meaning 'sharp' and 'dull'). Write a short poem which uses oxymorons.

3 'He is one – '

Write two lines in the same verse style as lines 141–50 to complete Helena's real thoughts after line 152.

4 'Baser stars'

In lines 155–61 Helena again reflects on how low her social status is in comparison with Bertram's. Keep this in mind as you read on. How would you make sure your audience was aware that Helena was considered of inferior status in the household of Rossillion?

Marry By St Mary
ill sinfully
gloss newness
vendible saleable
brooch and the toothpick ornaments worn in the hat
wear not now are out of fashion

phoenix mythical bird, born out of fire
dulcet soothing
adoptious christendoms . . . gossips christenings of adopted children with blind ('blinking') Cupid as godfather

PAROLLES Let me see. Marry, ill, to like him that ne'er it likes. 'Tis 130
a commodity will lose the gloss with lying; the longer kept, the less
worth. Off with't while 'tis vendible. Answer the time of request.
Virginity, like an old courtier, wears her cap out of fashion; richly
suited, but unsuitable: just like the brooch and the toothpick, which
wear not now. Your date is better in your pie and your porridge 135
than in your cheek; and your virginity, your old virginity, is like
one of our French withered pears: it looks ill, it eats drily. Marry,
'tis a withered pear; it was formerly better; marry, yet 'tis a
withered pear! Will you anything with it?

HELENA Not my virginity yet: 140
There shall your master have a thousand loves,
A mother, and a mistress, and a friend,
A phoenix, captain, and an enemy,
A guide, a goddess, and a sovereign,
A counsellor, a traitress, and a dear;   145
His humble ambition, proud humility,
His jarring, concord, and his discord, dulcet,
His faith, his sweet disaster; with a world
Of pretty, fond, adoptious christendoms
That blinking Cupid gossips. Now shall he –   150
I know not what he shall. God send him well!
The court's a learning-place, and he is one –

PAROLLES What one, i'faith?

HELENA That I wish well. 'Tis pity –

PAROLLES What's pity?   155

HELENA That wishing well had not a body in't
Which might be felt; that we, the poorer born,
Whose baser stars do shut us up in wishes,
Might with effects of them follow our friends
And show what we alone must think, which never   160
Returns us thanks.

Enter PAGE

PAGE Monsieur Parolles, my lord calls for you.   [*Exit*]

PAROLLES Little Helen, farewell. If I can remember thee, I will think
of thee at court.

HELENA Monsieur Parolles, you were born under a charitable star.   165

PAROLLES Under Mars I.

Helena mocks Parolles for being a coward. He gives her his advice before leaving to follow Bertram to court. Helena determines to do something positive to win Bertram.

---

1 Astrology: the 'fated sky' (in groups of four)

Parolles claims that being born under the star sign of Mars makes him a brave soldier. Do you read your horoscope, or do you make fun of such things, as Helena does in lines 166–72? Talk together about how much value you think should be placed on horoscopes. Many famous and powerful people regularly consult astrologers. Does this increase or lessen your respect for them?

2 'I cannot answer thee acutely' (in pairs)

Even though Parolles cannot answer Helena 'acutely', he is not lost for a reply (lines 179–86). Try at least four different ways of delivering these lines to suggest Parolles' personality. On the evidence you have so far, decide which one is the most likely.

3 A change of mood (in pairs)

Helena's cheerfully bawdy conversation with Parolles is framed by her two soliloquies. Read through the soliloquy opposite two or three times, speaking alternate sentences. Then turn back to page 7 and read that soliloquy through to refresh your memory.

Talk about the change in Helena's mood between the two soliloquies. What do you think has caused the change?

4 How should she speak?

Try out at least four ways of delivering Helena's soliloquy, for example: directly to the audience, to herself, to a portrait of Bertram, to a mirror.... Decide which way of speaking is the most appropriate.

---

predominant a favourable influence
retrograde an unfavourable influence
of a good wing enables you to run away (but also a comment on Parolles' clothes)

wear fashion, style
naturalise familiarise, teach
makes thee away destroys you
fated sky fateful stars
like likes similar natures

HELENA I especially think, under Mars.

PAROLLES Why under Mars?

HELENA The wars hath so kept you under that you must needs be born
under Mars.   170

PAROLLES When he was predominant.

HELENA When he was retrograde, I think rather.

PAROLLES Why think you so?

HELENA You go so much backward when you fight.

PAROLLES That's for advantage.   175

HELENA So is running away when fear proposes the safety. But the
composition that your valour and fear makes in you is a virtue of
a good wing, and I like the wear well.

PAROLLES I am so full of businesses I cannot answer thee acutely. I
will return perfect courtier, in the which my instruction shall serve 180
to naturalise thee, so thou wilt be capable of a courtier's counsel
and understand what advice shall thrust upon thee; else thou diest
in thine unthankfulness, and thine ignorance makes thee away.
Farewell. When thou hast leisure, say thy prayers; when thou hast
none, remember thy friends. Get thee a good husband, and use him 185
as he uses thee. So, farewell.   [*Exit*]

HELENA Our remedies oft in ourselves do lie,
Which we ascribe to heaven. The fated sky
Gives us free scope; only doth backward pull
Our slow designs when we ourselves are dull.   190
What power is it which mounts my love so high?
That makes me see, and cannot feed mine eye?
The mightiest space in fortune nature brings
To join like likes, and kiss like native things.
Impossible be strange attempts to those   195
That weigh their pains in sense, and do suppose
What hath been cannot be. Who ever strove
To show her merit that did miss her love?
The king's disease – my project may deceive me,
But my intents are fixed and will not leave me.   *Exit* 200

The King and his lords discuss the war between Florence and Siena. The King decides not to support Florence, but to allow his lords to fight for either side. He welcomes Bertram to court.

1 The entrance of the King (in groups of six or seven)

The illness of the King is very important to the plot. With one person as director, work out how you would show the King's illness on his first entrance with his courtiers. Act out your version and justify your group's ideas to the rest of the class.

2 The Italian wars

Italy was composed of a number of City States, some of them very wealthy and important in world affairs. They were frequently at war, and mercenaries (freelance soldiers) fought for any side that would pay them. The King appears not to mind whether his nobles fight for Florence or Siena ('freely have they leave/To stand on either part'). The Second Lord Dumaine feels that it would be a good 'nursery' for French lords who are inexperienced in battle but are very keen to fight ('sick/For breathing and exploit').

What do you think of the idea of war being a desirable way of keeping young men occupied? Make suggestions for suitable alternatives to such military service.

Senoys people of Siena
by th'ears quarrelling
cousin fellow sovereign
Austria Duke of Austria
move ask
Prejudicates prejudges

amplest credence total belief
mean to . . . service to fight in the
  war in Tuscany (Italy)
breathing exercise
curious carefully

ACT 1 SCENE 2
Paris The King's palace

Trumpet fanfare Enter the KING OF FRANCE *with letters, the* FIRST *and* SECOND LORDS *Dumaine and several attendants*

KING The Florentines and Senoys are by th'ears,
　　　Have fought with equal fortune, and continue
　　　A braving war.
FIRST LORD　　　　　So 'tis reported, sir.
KING Nay, 'tis most credible. We here receive it
　　　A certainty, vouched from our cousin Austria,　　　　　5
　　　With caution, that the Florentine will move us
　　　For speedy aid; wherein our dearest friend
　　　Prejudicates the business, and would seem
　　　To have us make denial.
FIRST LORD　　　　　　　　His love and wisdom,
　　　Approved so to your majesty, may plead　　　　　10
　　　For amplest credence.
KING　　　　　　　　He hath armed our answer,
　　　And Florence is denied before he comes.
　　　Yet for our gentlemen that mean to see
　　　The Tuscan service, freely have they leave
　　　To stand on either part.
SECOND LORD　　　　　It well may serve　　　　　15
　　　A nursery to our gentry, who are sick
　　　For breathing and exploit.
KING　　　　　　　　What's he comes here?

Enter BERTRAM, LAFEW, *and* PAROLLES

FIRST LORD It is the Count Rossillion, my good lord,
　　　Young Bertram.
KING　　　　　　　　Youth, thou bear'st thy father's face;
　　　Frank nature, rather curious than in haste,　　　　　20
　　　Hath well composed thee. Thy father's moral parts
　　　Mayst thou inherit too! Welcome to Paris.
BERTRAM My thanks and duty are your majesty's.

The King talks of his memories of Bertram's father. The King compares young men of his own court unfavourably with the late Count of Rossillion.

1 The Count of Rossillion – the servants' view

Using the King's lines 24–48, script a short scene where, just after his death, several of the late Count's servants discuss his qualities.

2 The good old days (in groups of six to eight)

The King thinks that young men were wittier and braver in his younger days than they are now. How far do you feel this is a typical reaction of the older generation?

One person reads the King's speech, pausing at the end of each sentence. During the pauses, the other members of the group, as young courtiers, voice their responses.

The King surrounded by his courtiers, Royal Shakespeare Company, 1992.

---

corporal soundness physical, bodily health

Till ... unnoted until they no longer notice when they themselves are being taunted

Who were below those who were below him in rank

copy example

goers backward followers of the past

So in approof ... speech your words confirm the truth of his epitaph

KING I would I had that corporal soundness now
      As when thy father and myself in friendship   25
      First tried our soldiership! He did look far
      Into the service of the time, and was
      Discipled of the bravest. He lasted long,
      But on us both did haggish age steal on,
      And wore us out of act. It much repairs me   30
      To talk of your good father. In his youth
      He had the wit which I can well observe
      Today in our young lords; but they may jest
      Till their own scorn return to them unnoted
      Ere they can hide their levity in honour.   35
      So like a courtier, contempt nor bitterness
      Were in his pride or sharpness; if they were,
      His equal had awaked them, and his honour,
      Clock to itself, knew the true minute when
      Exception bid him speak, and at this time   40
      His tongue obeyed his hand. Who were below him
      He used as creatures of another place,
      And bowed his eminent top to their low ranks,
      Making them proud of his humility,
      In their poor praise he humbled. Such a man   45
      Might be a copy to these younger times;
      Which followed well, would demonstrate them now
      But goers backward.
BERTRAM   His good remembrance, sir,
      Lies richer in your thoughts than on his tomb.
      So in approof lives not his epitaph   50
      As in your royal speech.

The King, wishing that he too were dead, continues his reminiscences of Bertram's father. He also remembers the late Gerard de Narbon and regrets that no doctor now living has been able to cure him.

1 'The catastrophe and heel of pastime'

Think of an equally colourful and memorable phrase as an alternative for line 57, which is a striking way of saying 'when he had finished some game or sport'.

2 Working for the hive

In lines 65–7, the King compares himself to a bee. The Elizabethans thought that the queen bee was actually a king, so this makes the King's metaphor more striking. Would you want the King to say these lines angrily, or bitterly, or sadly, or in some other way?

3 'I fill a place, I know't' (in pairs)

SECOND LORD   You're loved, sir;
    They that least lend it you shall lack you first.
KING   I fill a place, I know't.

Take one part each and learn these lines. Face one another and speak them. Turn away and write continuously for three minutes all the thoughts that occur to you. Turn back to your partner and read what you have written. Say your lines again, and talk about how this activity helps your understanding and performance.

This is an activity used by actors to help them explore a character's thoughts. Try it on other pairs of lines.

4 Exit the King (in pairs)

How would you want the King to say his final lines to bring out the irony of his personification of 'Nature and sickness'? In one production the King was wheeled off in a wheelchair. Talk together about how you would have the King leave the stage.

---

plausive pleasing
grafted planted deeply
melancholy seriousness
snuff suffocation

apprehensive over-hasty
**Mere fathers of their
    garments** only about new fashions
constancies serious intentions

KING Would I were with him. He would always say –
        Methinks I hear him now; his plausive words
        He scattered not in ears, but grafted them,
        To grow there and to bear – 'Let me not live' –   55
        This his good melancholy oft began,
        On the catastrophe and heel of pastime,
        When it was out – 'Let me not live', quoth he,
        'After my flame lacks oil, to be the snuff
        Of younger spirits, whose apprehensive senses   60
        All but new things disdain; whose judgements are
        Mere fathers of their garments; whose constancies
        Expire before their fashions.' This he wished.
        I, after him, do after him wish too,
        Since I nor wax nor honey can bring home,   65
        I quickly were dissolvèd from my hive,
        To give some labourers room.
SECOND LORD   You're loved, sir;
        They that least lend it you shall lack you first.
KING I fill a place, I know't. How long is't, count,   70
        Since the physician at your father's died?
        He was much famed.
BERTRAM   Some six months since, my lord.
KING If he were living, I would try him yet –
        Lend me an arm – the rest have worn me out   75
        With several applications. Nature and sickness
        Debate it at their leisure. Welcome, count,
        My son's no dearer.
BERTRAM   Thank your majesty.
                                        [*Exeunt*] *Flourish*

The Countess asks Rinaldo about Helena, but is diverted by Lavatch who asks for her support in his proposed marriage to Isbel.

Lavatch can be a difficult character to present because he has no equivalent in a modern household. Study these illustrations from past productions. Which aspects of his personality are the directors presenting in each?

calendar public record
to . . . world to marry
woman serving woman

Isbel's case matter to be decided
  (also, vagina)
barnes children (bairns)
out a'friends without friends

ACT I SCENE 3
The Palace of Rossillion

Enter the COUNTESS, RINALDO and LAVATCH

COUNTESS I will now hear. What say you of this gentlewoman?

RINALDO Madam, the care I have had to even your content, I wish
    might be found in the calendar of my past endeavours, for then we
    wound our modesty, and make foul the clearness of our deservings,
    when of ourselves we publish them. 5

COUNTESS What does this knave here? Get you gone, sirrah. The
    complaints I have heard of you I do not all believe; 'tis my slowness
    that I do not, for I know you lack not folly to commit them, and
    have ability enough to make such knaveries yours.

LAVATCH 'Tis not unknown to you, madam, I am a poor fellow. 10

COUNTESS Well, sir.

LAVATCH No, madam, 'tis not so well that I am poor, though many
    of the rich are damned, but if I may have your ladyship's good will
    to go to the world, Isbel the woman and I will do as we may.

COUNTESS Wilt thou needs be a beggar? 15

LAVATCH I do beg your good will in this case.

COUNTESS In what case?

LAVATCH In Isbel's case and mine own. Service is no heritage, and I
    think I shall never have the blessing of God till I have issue a'my
    body; for they say barnes are blessings. 20

COUNTESS Tell me thy reason why thou wilt marry.

LAVATCH My poor body, madam, requires it. I am driven on by the
    flesh, and he must needs go that the devil drives.

COUNTESS Is this all your worship's reason?

LAVATCH Faith, madam, I have other holy reasons, such as they are. 25

COUNTESS May the world know them?

LAVATCH I have been, madam, a wicked creature, as you and all flesh
    and blood are, and indeed I do marry that I may repent.

COUNTESS Thy marriage, sooner than thy wickedness.

LAVATCH I am out a'friends, madam, and I hope to have friends for my 30
    wife's sake.

COUNTESS Such friends are thine enemies, knave.

Lavatch tells the Countess that he prefers friends who relieve him of the drudgery of having sex with his wife. He sings a song about Helen of Troy, and comments cynically on women's faithfulness.

1 Marriage = adultery? (in pairs)

Read Lavatch's lines 33–43, speaking a sentence each in turn. Does he believe what he is saying, or is he joking? Talk about how you, as directors, would want the audience to react to his ideas about marriage.

2 'There's yet one good in ten'

Lavatch's cynicism (line 64) is an echo of Parolles' speeches about virginity. He sings about Helen of Troy, popularly supposed to have been an immoral woman, and he deliberately changes the words of the old song to suggest that only one woman in ten is virtuous.

Imagine that Isbel complains to the Countess about Lavatch. Using lines 55–75, present her complaint in a letter or in an improvisation.

3 Isbel – should she be here? (in pairs)

Isbel does not say anything during the play, nor is her character included in any of the stage directions. However, her actual appearance on-stage offers lots of potential for comedy. Would you want an Isbel in your cast? Talk together about what kind of person she might be, and what she might do if she were on-stage.

4 Rinaldo the steward

You are playing Rinaldo. Work out what you would do while Lavatch and the Countess are talking. Rinaldo's actions should help the audience to understand how he feels about Lavatch's behaviour.

---

ears ploughs
team yoked oxen
leave to in permission to harvest
cuckold deceived husband
Charbon (nickname for) Puritan
Poysam (nickname for) Catholic
jowl knock
calumnious slanderous

by kind according to its nature
sackèd destroyed
tithe-woman one woman in ten (parsons were allowed a tenth of all produce)
quoth'a? did you say?
ore only
mend the lottery improve the odds

LAVATCH Y'are shallow, madam, in great friends, for the knaves come
to do that for me which I am a-weary of. He that ears my land spares
my team, and gives me leave to in the crop. If I be his cuckold,   35
he's my drudge. He that comforts my wife is the cherisher of my
flesh and blood; he that cherishes my flesh and blood loves my flesh
and blood; he that loves my flesh and blood is my friend: *ergo*, he
that kisses my wife is my friend. If men could be contented to be
what they are, there were no fear in marriage, for young Charbon   40
the puritan and old Poysam the papist, howsome'er their hearts are
severed in religion, their heads are both one: they may jowl horns
together like any deer i'th'herd.

COUNTESS Wilt thou ever be a foul-mouthed and calumnious knave?

LAVATCH A prophet I, madam, and I speak the truth the next way: 45
    For I the ballad will repeat,
      Which men full true shall find:
    Your marriage comes by destiny,
      Your cuckoo sings by kind.

COUNTESS Get you gone, sir, I'll talk with you more anon.   50

RINALDO May it please you, madam, that he bid Helen come to you.
Of her I am to speak.

COUNTESS Sirrah, tell my gentlewoman I would speak with her – Helen,
I mean.

LAVATCH   'Was this fair face the cause', quoth she,   55
      'Why the Grecians sackèd Troy?
    Fond done, done fond,
      Was this King Priam's joy?'
    With that she sighèd as she stood,
    With that she sighèd as she stood,   60
      And gave this sentence then:
    'Among nine bad if one be good,
    Among nine bad if one be good,
      There's yet one good in ten.'

COUNTESS What, one good in ten? You corrupt the song, sirrah.   65

LAVATCH One good woman in ten, madam, which is a purifying
a'th'song. Would God would serve the world so all the year! we'd
find no fault with the tithe-woman if I were the parson. One in ten,
quoth'a? And we might have a good woman born but ore every
blazing star or at an earthquake, 'twould mend the lottery well; a   70
man may draw his heart out ere 'a pluck one.

COUNTESS You'll be gone, sir knave, and do as I command you?

23

Rinaldo tells the Countess that he has overheard Helena speaking about her love for Bertram. This confirms what the Countess has already thought likely. She remembers that young love can be painful.

1 'I am going, forsooth' (in pairs)

The Countess asks Lavatch to fetch Helena (line 54). Lavatch puts off doing as he's told, and the Countess has to remind him (line 72). He makes a joke about wearing the 'surplice of humility over the black gown of a big heart'. This is a reference to the puritans, who wore their black Geneva (Calvinist) gown under the lawful white robe of the Church of England. Talk together about how you would want Lavatch to say lines 74–6, and whether you would add any stage business (an unspoken threat from Rinaldo, perhaps?) to finally get Lavatch to leave.

2 'Her father bequeathed her to me' (in pairs)

Improvise the scene between the Countess and the dying Gerard de Narbon, when he asks her to take care of Helena after his death (line 79). This situation requires sensitivity on both sides. What exactly does he ask, and what does she promise to do for Helena?

3 Rinaldo's motives

Rinaldo has overheard Helena worrying about the social class difference between Bertram and herself (lines 83–94). What do you think are his motives for telling the Countess what he has heard? Justify your answers using the script.

4 Helena's missing soliloquy

What Rinaldo describes in lines 83–94 does not match either of the soliloquies that Helena has spoken. Using the hints given by Rinaldo, write the soliloquy that he overheard. Try using iambic pentameter (page 183 will help).

---

bequeathed her to me gave her into my care
stranger sense to the ears of anyone else
estates ranks, positions
Diana goddess of virginity

touch tone
sithence since
Stall . . . bosom keep quiet about this
blood passion
impressed stamped by a seal

LAVATCH That man should be at woman's command, and yet no hurt
  done! Though honesty be no puritan, yet it will do no hurt; it will
  wear the surplice of humility over the black gown of a big heart.   75
  I am going, forsooth. The business is for Helen to come hither.
                                                                  Exit
COUNTESS Well, now.
RINALDO I know, madam, you love your gentlewoman entirely.
COUNTESS Faith, I do. Her father bequeathed her to me, and she
  herself, without other advantage, may lawfully make title to as much   80
  love as she finds. There is more owing her than is paid, and more
  shall be paid her than she'll demand.
RINALDO Madam, I was very late more near her than I think she wished
  me. Alone she was, and did communicate to herself her own words
  to her own ears; she thought, I dare vow for her, they touched not   85
  any stranger sense. Her matter was, she loved your son. Fortune,
  she said, was no goddess, that had put such difference betwixt their
  two estates; Love no god, that would not extend his might only
  where qualities were level; [Diana no] queen of virgins, that would
  suffer her poor knight surprised without rescue in the first assault   90
  or ransom afterward. This she delivered in the most bitter touch
  of sorrow that e'er I heard virgin exclaim in, which I held my duty
  speedily to acquaint you withal, sithence in the loss that may
  happen, it concerns you something to know it.
COUNTESS You have discharged this honestly, keep it to yourself. Many 95
  likelihoods informed me of this before, which hung so tottering in
  the balance that I could neither believe nor misdoubt. Pray you
  leave me. Stall this in your bosom, and I thank you for your honest
  care. I will speak with you further anon.
                                          Exit [Rinaldo, the] Steward

          Enter HELENA

          Even so it was with me when I was young.   100
          If ever we are nature's, these are ours. This thorn
          Doth to our rose of youth rightly belong;
          Our blood to us, this to our blood is born.
          It is the show and seal of nature's truth,
          Where love's strong passion is impressed in youth.   105
          By our remembrances of days foregone,
          Such were our faults, or then we thought them none.
          Her eye is sick on't; I observe her now.

The Countess urges Helena to look on her as a mother. Helena is unwilling to do so, stressing her lowly social status. She hints at her love for Bertram.

---

1 Shakespeare – the actor's playwright (in groups of three)

Act out the conversation between Helena and the Countess (lines 109–66), with one person as director. Identify and use Shakespeare's 'buried' stage directions for Helena.

Choose a line from the script opposite as a caption for this photograph. Compare and justify your choice of line with other students' choices.

---

enwombèd born
choice . . . seeds adopted children become like their adoptive parents
curd curdle

Iris rainbow (Iris was the goddess of the rainbow)
note title
vassal slave or subject

26

HELENA What is your pleasure, madam?

COUNTESS   You know, Helen,
   I am a mother to you.   110

HELENA Mine honourable mistress.

COUNTESS   Nay, a mother,
      Why not a mother? When I said 'a mother',
      Methought you saw a serpent. What's in 'mother',
      That you start at it? I say I am your mother,
      And put you in the catalogue of those   115
      That were enwombèd mine. 'Tis often seen
      Adoption strives with nature, and choice breeds
      A native slip to us from foreign seeds.
      You ne'er oppressed me with a mother's groan,
      Yet I express to you a mother's care.   120
      God's mercy, maiden! does it curd thy blood
      To say I am thy mother? What's the matter,
      That this distempered messenger of wet,
      The many-coloured Iris, rounds thine eye?
      – Why, that you are my daughter?

HELENA   That I am not.   125

COUNTESS I say I am your mother.

HELENA   Pardon, madam;
      The Count Rossillion cannot be my brother;
      I am from humble, he from honoured name;
      No note upon my parents, his all noble.
      My master, my dear lord he is, and I   130
      His servant live, and will his vassal die.
      He must not be my brother.

COUNTESS   Nor I your mother?

HELENA You are my mother, madam; would you were –
      So that my lord your son were not my brother –
      Indeed my mother! Or were you both our mothers, 135
      I care no more for than I do for heaven,
      So I were not his sister. Can 't no other,
      But, I your daughter, he must be my brother?

The Countess can see how Helena feels from the way in which she reacts.
Helena finally admits that she loves Bertram.

1 What's the mood here? (in pairs)

a Key words

Read lines 139–57 taking turns to read up to a punctuation mark.
Change over and read the lines again. Talk about which you think are
the key words. Choose five which you feel express the tone of the
Countess's speech.

b The Countess's mood

Act out lines 155–63. Do you think the Countess's mood is angry . . .
cajoling . . . tender . . . ? Experiment with different ways of speaking
the lines.

c Helena's replies

How do you think Helena says her three short lines: abruptly . . .
humbly . . . with a long pause . . . ? How do the different ways of
speaking the lines affect your understanding of the dialogue?

2 What happens next?

Before you turn the page: how do you think the Countess will react to
Helena's confession?

My fear . . . fondness! my
  suspicion has discovered your
  foolishness (or love – fondness has
  both meanings)
head source
gross/grossly obvious/obviously
Invention ability to lie

wound a goodly clew made a
  tangle of things (a 'clew' is a ball of
  twine)
avail good, benefit
Go not about don't evade the
  question
appeached given you away

COUNTESS Yes, Helen, you might be my daughter-in-law.
    God shield you mean it not! 'Daughter' and 'mother'   140
    So strive upon your pulse. What, pale again?
    My fear hath catched your fondness! Now I see
    The mystery of your loneliness, and find
    Your salt tears' head. Now to all sense 'tis gross:
    You love my son. Invention is ashamed,   145
    Against the proclamation of thy passion,
    To say thou dost not: therefore tell me true,
    But tell me then 'tis so; for look, thy cheeks
    Confess it, t'one to th'other, and thine eyes
    See it so grossly shown in thy behaviours   150
    That in their kind they speak it. Only sin
    And hellish obstinacy tie thy tongue,
    That truth should be suspected. Speak, is't so?
    If it be so, you have wound a goodly clew;
    If it be not, forswear't; howe'er, I charge thee,   155
    As heaven shall work in me for thine avail,
    To tell me truly.
HELENA   Good madam, pardon me!
COUNTESS Do you love my son?
HELENA   Your pardon, noble mistress!
COUNTESS Love you my son?
HELENA   Do not you love him, madam?
COUNTESS Go not about; my love hath in't a bond   160
    Whereof the world takes note. Come, come, disclose
    The state of your affection, for your passions
    Have to the full appeached.
HELENA   Then I confess
    Here on my knee, before high heaven and you,
    That before you, and next unto high heaven,   165
    I love your son.

Helena speaks of her devotion to Bertram, which is like a religion to her. She wants to go to Paris to try out her father's remedies on the King.

1 Echoes of love (in pairs)

Read Helena's lines 167–89 twice, changing speaker at each punctuation mark. For your third reading, one person reads the speech and the other person echoes every reference to love. Do you think that Helena expects the Countess's sympathy?

2 Gerard de Narbon – his 'notes'

Helena's father has collected remedies and prescriptions for all diseases. You have come into possession of his notes and intend to sell the medicines. Using lines 193–202, write your first advertisement for these wonderful cures.

Observ. XCVIII.

Dixwel Brunt of Pillerton, aged 3 years, had a Tumor of the Navil, out of which broke five long Worms out of a little hole like a Fistula; the Nurse pulled out four dead, but the fifth was somewhat alive, the fore-part not moving, the hinder part stirred, as witnessed the Nurse, Father, Mother, and Maid. The Tumor being hard, I appointed a Platter of Hony to be applied. The same day was given a Suppository of Honey, but no Worms appeared. The next day was applied a Cataplasm framed of green Wormwood, beat with the Gall of an Ox, and boyled. There was given a Suppository. After these the Navil was cured, and he lived.

A remedy for a fistula. Dr John Hall was married to Shakespeare's daughter, Susanna. He kept a casebook of many of his successful cures, and had it published. The unfortunate child treated by Dr Hall for a fistula lived at Pillerton, a village a few miles south-east of Stratford-upon-Avon.

---

presumptuous suit forward proposal
desert deserving
captious and intenible huge and ever-emptying
lack . . . still still have enough to squander
Indian-like like a pagan

encounter do battle
Dian Diana (goddess of chastity)
general sovereignty universal cure
in heedfull'st . . . them to keep them very carefully for use
faculties inclusive comprehensive powers
in note generally known

My friends were poor but honest, so's my love.
Be not offended, for it hurts not him
That he is loved of me; I follow him not
By any token of presumptuous suit,   170
Nor would I have him till I do deserve him,
Yet never know how that desert should be.
I know I love in vain, strive against hope;
Yet in this captious and intenible sieve
I still pour in the waters of my love   175
And lack not to lose still. Thus Indian-like,
Religious in mine error, I adore
The sun, that looks upon his worshipper,
But knows of him no more. My dearest madam,
Let not your hate encounter with my love   180
For loving where you do; but if yourself,
Whose agèd honour cites a virtuous youth,
Did ever in so true a flame of liking
Wish chastely, and love dearly, that your Dian
Was both herself and Love, O then give pity   185
To her whose state is such that cannot choose
But lend and give where she is sure to lose;
That seeks not to find that her search implies,
But riddle-like lives sweetly where she dies.
COUNTESS Had you not lately an intent – speak truly –   190
  To go to Paris?
HELENA   Madam, I had.
COUNTESS   Wherefore? tell true.
HELENA I will tell truth, by grace itself I swear.
  You know my father left me some prescriptions
  Of rare and proved effects, such as his reading
  And manifest experience had collected   195
  For general sovereignty; and that he willed me
  In heedfull'st reservation to bestow them,
  As notes whose faculties inclusive were
  More than they were in note. Amongst the rest,
  There is a remedy, approved, set down,   200
  To cure the desperate languishings whereof
  The king is rendered lost.

Helena admits that her real reason for going to Paris is to see Bertram, rather than to cure the King. Although she is sceptical of Helena's chances of success in curing the King's illness, the Countess allows her to try.

1 Off to Paris (in pairs)

The Countess wonders what kind of reception Helena will receive from the King. Talk together about how you imagine this encounter will go. Use what you have learned about social class and the personality of the King to help you. Compare your version with what actually happens in Act 2 when you read on.

2 'Th'luckiest stars in heaven' (in pairs)

During Act 1, there have been several references to stars, fate and heaven. See how many you can find, and begin a collage of quotations which you can add to as you read on.

3 'What I can help thee to thou shalt not miss'

Write the letter that the Countess sends to an old friend, Lord Lafew, at court, encouraging him to give Helena every support in her attempt to cure the King.

Haply by chance
schools universities
Embowelled emptied
doctrine medical knowledge

left off abandoned
receipt prescription
sanctified blessed

COUNTESS   This was your motive
        For Paris, was it? Speak.
HELENA My lord your son made me to think of this;
        Else Paris, and the medicine, and the king,   205
        Had from the conversation of my thoughts
        Haply been absent then.
COUNTESS   But think you, Helen,
        If you should tender your supposèd aid,
        He would receive it? He and his physicians
        Are of a mind; he, that they cannot help him,   210
        They, that they cannot help. How shall they credit
        A poor unlearnèd virgin, when the schools,
        Embowelled of their doctrine, have left off
        The danger to itself?
HELENA   There's something in't
        More than my father's skill, which was the great'st   215
        Of his profession, that his good receipt
        Shall for my legacy be sanctified
        By th'luckiest stars in heaven, and would your honour
        But give me leave to try success, I'd venture
        The well-lost life of mine on his grace's cure   220
        By such a day, an hour.
COUNTESS   Dost thou believe't?
HELENA Ay, madam, knowingly.
COUNTESS Why, Helen, thou shalt have my leave and love,
        Means and attendants, and my loving greetings
        To those of mine in court. I'll stay at home   225
        And pray God's blessing into thy attempt.
        Be gone tomorrow, and be sure of this,
        What I can help thee to thou shalt not miss.
                                              Exeunt

Looking back at Act 1
Activities for groups or individuals

1 Setting the tone

A dramatically effective way of setting the tone for a production is to precede the first act with a dumb-show. Choose from one of the following or decide on an idea of your own:

- the funeral of the late Count of Rossillion
- the funeral of Gerard de Narbon
- the illness of the King
- the war in Italy.

Make the dumb-show as theatrical as you can, using mime and possibly music.

2 Setting the scene in Rossillion

Design the set for the opening scene. Talk together about which props you would use to give a visual image to your audience, and how the set could be used to create a particular atmosphere. A very swift change is needed to the King's court in Paris. What changes would you make then? Try to avoid a blackout and a complete change of set – you will lose the attention of the audience.

3 *All's Well* – the novel

Try writing the opening of *All's Well* as a novel. You could base the style of the novel on something that you already know, for example: a romance, a mystery or a gothic horror story.

4 Seduction – two literary traditions

Parolles' ideas about getting rid of virginity are part of a widespread tradition of mock heroic poems, which are about trying to get a girl into bed as quickly as possible. Find a copy of *To His Coy Mistress* by Andrew Marvell or *The Flea* by John Donne, and compare them with Parolles' lines in Act 1 Scene 1.

There was an equally popular tradition in which women were frequently the subject of courtly love poetry, which elevated them and exaggerated their beauty and virtues. Shakespeare undermines the tradition of inflated language to describe his lady's beauty in his sonnet 130 'My mistress' eyes are nothing like the sun'. This convention led to problems if women did not entirely live up to the elevated (and passive) position assigned to them. There was no middle way: women were either virtuous or whores (as shown in the trouble Diana has in Act 5, and by Hero's problems in *Much Ado About Nothing*).

5 'I am from humble, he from honoured name'

One of the main themes of *All's Well* is the distinction between the various social classes. Helena is all too aware of the impossibility of her marrying Bertram, even though her father was a famous doctor. Lavatch has to ask the Countess for permission to marry Isbel, and Parolles' precise social position is not made explicit in Act 1. Arrange all the characters that you have met in Act 1 according to their social rank. Make a note of your rank order to compare with your ideas when you read activity 8 on page 185.

6 Love or lust?

Talk together about the different attitudes towards the relationship between the sexes expressed in Act 1:

a Helena's first soliloquy (Scene 1, lines 67–86) about her love for Bertram is romantic and idealistic.

b Her bawdy chat with Parolles (Scene 1, lines 94–139) is much more down-to-earth. It is about the difficulties of defending virginity against pestering men.

c Lavatch only talks about sex. He claims he is 'driven on by the flesh' (Scene 3, line 22), and therefore must get married.

d Helena speaks of her love for Bertram (Scene 3, lines 163–89) as though he were her god.

The King takes leave of the young lords who are going to war. They wish him good health, but he does not expect to recover. He warns them about the seductive girls in Italy.

1 What advice?

Shakespeare often begins acts and scenes in the middle of a conversation. In line 1, the King has been giving advice ('warlike principles') to the young lords who are leaving to go to the Florentine wars. What advice do you think he has offered? Write a speech of about four lines for the King – possibly practical advice about caring for weapons – which he can speak quietly as he goes onto the stage. This would make it easier for your actors to enter with confidence.

2 Grouping (in groups of eight to ten)

Large groups on-stage can be a director's nightmare. Take turns to direct the entrance and positioning of your actors for lines 1–7. For example, line 2 could suggest two groups of soldiers, one group leaving for Florence and one for Siena. Talk about the difficulties, then devise a tableau for lines 1–2.

3 Lock up your daughters? (in small groups)

Typically for this time, the King warns the young men not to be seduced by the Italian girls. Do you think the King should be warning his soldiers, or the Italian parents their daughters? It seems inevitable that parents and other older people always want to warn the young. What do you think is the most important piece of advice you have ever been given about relationships with the opposite sex?

---

doth stretch expands
well-entered experienced
owes owns

bated wretched ones
questant seeker of honour
spark dashing young man

ACT 2 SCENE 1
Paris   The King's palace

Trumpet fanfare   Enter the KING, *the* FIRST *and* SECOND LORDS
Dumaine, some young lords, BERTRAM *and* PAROLLES

KING Farewell, young lords, these warlike principles
    Do not throw from you; and you, my lords, farewell.
    Share the advice betwixt you; if both gain all,
    The gift doth stretch itself as 'tis received,
    And is enough for both.
FIRST LORD   'Tis our hope, sir,   5
    After well-entered soldiers, to return
    And find your grace in health.
KING No, no, it cannot be; and yet my heart
    Will not confess he owes the malady
    That doth my life besiege. Farewell, young lords,   10
    Whether I live or die, be you the sons
    Of worthy Frenchmen. Let higher Italy
    (Those bated that inherit but the fall
    Of the last monarchy) see that you come
    Not to woo honour, but to wed it, when   15
    The bravest questant shrinks. Find what you seek,
    That fame may cry you loud. I say farewell.
FIRST LORD Health, at your bidding, serve your majesty!
KING Those girls of Italy, take heed of them.
    They say our French lack language to deny   20
    If they demand. Beware of being captives
    Before you serve.
BOTH LORDS   Our hearts receive your warnings.
KING Farewell. – Come hither to me.
FIRST LORD O my sweet lord, that you will stay behind us!
PAROLLES 'Tis not his fault, the spark.
SECOND LORD   O, 'tis brave wars!   25
PAROLLES Most admirable! I have seen those wars.

Bertram is annoyed that he has been ordered to remain behind because he is too young to go to war. Parolles boasts about wounding an Italian soldier called Captain Spurio.

1 'Too young'

Practise saying line 28 as meaningfully as possible, having at the back of your mind some time in your life when you were prevented from doing something because you were too young. Actors often use this technique of **emotion memory** to help them act more truthfully.

2 'Our parting is a tortured body' (in groups of eight to ten)

Present a tableau of the court at line 36. Your audience should be able to identify all the leading characters. You will need to consider the group around the King: Bertram, Parolles, the young lords, and possible attendants. How do you think each character feels about the future?

Notice how Shakespeare shifts the dramatic focus of the scene from the King to Bertram in line 23, and back again to the King at Lafew's entrance at line 57.

3 Circumlocution and tautology (in groups of three)

'Parole' is French for 'word', but it can also mean 'promise'; a prisoner who is 'on parole' has promised to abide by certain rules. 'Spurio' (line 41) is Italian for 'fake'. What does this suggest to you about Parolles' boasting? Parolles' name becomes more ironic as the play progresses.

In lines 48–54, Parolles uses more words than are really necessary, and repeats himself. How would you express what he means more concisely? Which group can use the fewest words?

---

kept a coil fussed
forehorse to a smock leading
  horse in a team driven by a woman
bought up sold out
lustrous shining spirits
metals swordsmen
cicatrice scar
sinister left

spacious ceremony elaborate
  politeness
list limit
wear . . . time are leaders of
  fashion
muster true gait behave in courtly
  manner
measure dance

BERTRAM I am commanded here, and kept a coil with,
    'Too young' and 'the next year' and ''tis too early'.
PAROLLES And thy mind stand to't, boy, steal away bravely.
BERTRAM I shall stay here the forehorse to a smock,   30
    Creaking my shoes on the plain masonry,
    Till honour be bought up, and no sword worn
    But one to dance with! By heaven, I'll steal away.
FIRST LORD There's honour in the theft.
PAROLLES   Commit it, count.
SECOND LORD I am your accessory, and so farewell.   35
BERTRAM I grow to you, and our parting is a tortured body.
FIRST LORD Farewell, captain.
SECOND LORD Sweet Monsieur Parolles!
PAROLLES Noble heroes! my sword and yours are kin. Good sparks and
    lustrous, a word, good metals: you shall find in the regiment of the   40
    Spinii one Captain Spurio, with his cicatrice, an emblem of war,
    here on his sinister cheek; it was this very sword entrenched it. Say
    to him I live, and observe his reports for me.
FIRST LORD We shall, noble captain.
PAROLLES Mars dote on you for his novices!   45
                                  [*Exeunt Lords*]
    What will ye do?
BERTRAM Stay: the king.
PAROLLES Use a more spacious ceremony to the noble lords; you have
    restrained yourself within the list of too cold an adieu. Be more
    expressive to them, for they wear themselves in the cap of the time,   50
    there do muster true gait; eat, speak, and move under the influence
    of the most received star, and though the devil lead the measure,
    such are to be followed. After them, and take a more dilated
    farewell.
BERTRAM And I will do so.   55
PAROLLES Worthy fellows, and like to prove most sinewy swordmen.
                                       Exeunt

*Lafew asks the King if he thinks he will be cured. When the King replies
'No', Lafew predicts wonders. He announces the arrival of 'Doctor' Helena
and praises her powers.*

1 Old friends (in pairs)

Though the King is far above
Lafew in rank, the two men are
able to talk together in a friendly,
joking manner. Present lines
57–88 to the rest of your group,
emphasising the humour without
forgetting the difference in status
of the two men.

Aesop's fable of *The Fox and the
Grapes*. A fox tried, without success,
to reach some grapes hanging from a
tree. He went off, comforting
himself by saying 'They weren't ripe
anyway'. Similarly, some men put
the blame on external
circumstances, when they are
actually failing through their own
lack of effort.

2 Miraculous medicine (in pairs)

Lines 69–74 list the wonderful powers that Lafew claims Helena's
medicine has. Consider each claim separately. Why do you think
Lafew makes such exaggerated claims?

---

pate head
canary Spanish dance
simple mere
araise King Pippen bring life to
  the long dead King Pepin

Charlemain Charlemagne (Holy
  Roman Emperor in AD 800)
light deliverance joking manner
admiration wonderful object
prologues introduces

Enter LAFEW. [*The* KING *comes forward*]

LAFEW [*Kneeling*] Pardon, my lord, for me and for my tidings.
KING I'll see thee to stand up.
LAFEW Then here's a man stands that has brought his pardon.
      I would you had kneeled, my lord, to ask me mercy,   60
      And that at my bidding you could so stand up.
KING I would I had, so I had broke thy pate,
      And asked thee mercy for't.
LAFEW   Good faith, across!
      But, my good lord, 'tis thus: you will be cured
      Of your infirmity?
KING   No.
LAFEW   O, will you eat   65
      No grapes, my royal fox? Yes, but you will
      My noble grapes, and if my royal fox
      Could reach them. I have seen a medicine
      That's able to breathe life into a stone,
      Quicken a rock, and make you dance canary   70
      With spritely fire and motion, whose simple touch
      Is powerful to araise King Pippen, nay,
      To give great Charlemain a pen in's hand
      And write to her a love-line.
KING   What her is this?
LAFEW Why, Doctor She! My lord, there's one arrived,   75
      If you will see her. Now by my faith and honour,
      If seriously I may convey my thoughts
      In this my light deliverance, I have spoke
      With one, that in her sex, her years, profession,
      Wisdom, and constancy, hath amazed me more   80
      Than I dare blame my weakness. Will you see her –
      For that is her demand – and know her business?
      That done, laugh well at me.
KING   Now, good Lafew,
      Bring in the admiration, that we with thee
      May spend our wonder too, or take off thine   85
      By wondering how thou took'st it.
LAFEW   Nay, I'll fit you,
      And not be all day neither.
               [*Goes to the door*]
KING Thus he his special nothing ever prologues.

Helena tells the King that she is the daughter of Gerard de Narbon and has a possible remedy for his illness. The King doubts whether this is likely.

---

1 'Cressid's uncle'

Cressida (line 93) is a character in one of the stories about the Trojan War. Shakespeare uses the story in his play *Troilus and Cressida*. Troilus, a Trojan prince, falls in love with Cressida. Troilus uses Cressida's uncle, Pandarus, as a go-between to enable him to meet and sleep with her. The word 'pandar', meaning 'pimp', comes from his name. Do you think that Lafew is having a mild sexual joke at the King's expense here, or is he making a bawdy insinuation about Helena?

2 Getting into the skin (in pairs)

A common rehearsal technique used by actors to get 'into the skin' of a role is to reduce each speech to single sentences.

Taking one part each, beginning at line 99 and continuing to the end of the scene, reduce each speech to a single sentence in your own words. Act out the resulting conversation, putting as much emphasis as possible on the emotion underlying each speech. Then go back to the script and read from line 99 again, trying to remember how you felt as you were saying your version. How does this activity illuminate your understanding of the action?

3 Stage directions

If you were directing Helena, how would you advise her to behave and move during lines 121–4?

The rather therefore
receipts prescriptions for medicines
triple eye third eye
appliance skill in treatment
leave abandon hope for
congregated college society of doctors

inaidable estate incurable condition
prostitute ... èmpirics to allow quack doctors to meddle with our incurable disease
dissever separate
office service
to ... again to take back with me

LAFEW Nay, come your ways.

Enter HELENA

KING   This haste hath wings indeed.
LAFEW Nay, come your ways;   90
    This is his majesty, say your mind to him.
    A traitor you do look like, but such traitors
    His majesty seldom fears. I am Cressid's uncle,
    That dare leave two together; fare you well.   *Exit*
KING Now, fair one, does your business follow us?   95
HELENA Ay, my good lord.
    Gerard de Narbon was my father,
    In what he did profess, well found.
KING   I knew him.
HELENA The rather will I spare my praises towards him,
    Knowing him is enough. On's bed of death   100
    Many receipts he gave me; chiefly one,
    Which as the dearest issue of his practice,
    And of his old experience th'only darling,
    He bade me store up, as a triple eye,
    Safer than mine own two, more dear. I have so,   105
    And hearing your high majesty is touched
    With that malignant cause wherein the honour
    Of my dear father's gift stands chief in power,
    I come to tender it, and my appliance,
    With all bound humbleness.
KING   We thank you, maiden,   110
    But may not be so credulous of cure,
    When our most learnèd doctors leave us, and
    The congregated college have concluded
    That labouring art can never ransom nature
    From her inaidable estate; I say we must not   115
    So stain our judgement, or corrupt our hope,
    To prostitute our past-cure malady
    To èmpirics, or to dissever so
    Our great self and our credit, to esteem
    A senseless help when help past sense we deem.   120
HELENA My duty then shall pay me for my pains.
    I will no more enforce mine office on you,
    Humbly entreating from your royal thoughts
    A modest one, to bear me back again.

Helena argues that apparent weakness can have great power. The King dismisses her offer of help, but she persists in claiming that she can cure him within two days.

1 Weakness *v* strength (in groups of three)

The argument Helena uses to try to convince the King is based on the common idea that it is not always the obviously powerful who succeed. This has parallels in the fables of *The Tortoise and the Hare* and *The Mouse and the Lion*. Which factors do you think make Helena weak in this society?

2 Rhyming couplets (in pairs)

Except for occasional lines, the rest of this scene is written in rhyming couplets. You can pick this up easily by speaking the last word of each line. What effect do you think this has on the rhythm of the words spoken by Helena and the King? Consider the rest of the scene together, reading one *line* each alternately, then reading again in *sense units* (meaningful sections, which may be longer than one line). Compare this with your readings of unrhymed speeches, for example lines 99–118 on the previous page.

3 The music of the spheres

The Royal Shakespeare Company's 1992 production used 'magical' music to accompany lines 156–64. Helena spoke the lines as though she were receiving inspiration from the heavens.

- If you were directing the play, how would you ensure that these lines create a special dramatic effect?
- From whom does Helena suggest that her complete confidence in her father's remedies comes? (Helena's lines 144–54 will help.)

---

set up your rest stake everything
shifts blows hot and cold
Proffers not took offers not accepted
Inspired . . . barred inspiration (breathed in from God) is forbidden by words (breathed out by the King)

square . . . shows judge by appearances
horses of the sun horses that pull the chariot of Apollo (the sun god)
torcher torch-bearer
diurnal daily
Hesperus the evening star (Venus)
glass hour-glass

KING I cannot give thee less, to be called grateful.   125
        Thou thought'st to help me, and such thanks I give
        As one near death to those that wish him live.
        But what at full I know, thou know'st no part,
        I knowing all my peril, thou no art.
HELENA What I can do can do no hurt to try,   130
        Since you set up your rest 'gainst remedy.
        He that of greatest works is finisher
        Oft does them by the weakest minister:
        So holy writ in babes hath judgement shown,
        When judges have been babes; great floods have flown   135
        From simple sources; and great seas have dried
        When miracles have by the great'st been denied.
        Oft expectation fails, and most oft there
        Where most it promises; and oft it hits
        Where hope is coldest, and despair most shifts.   140
KING I must not hear thee; fare thee well, kind maid,
        Thy pains not used must by thyself be paid.
        Proffers not took reap thanks for their reward.
HELENA Inspired merit so by breath is barred.
        It is not so with Him that all things knows   145
        As 'tis with us that square our guess by shows;
        But most it is presumption in us when
        The help of heaven we count the act of men.
        Dear sir, to my endeavours give consent,
        Of heaven, not me, make an experiment.   150
        I am not an impostor that proclaim
        Myself against the level of mine aim,
        But know I think, and think I know most sure,
        My art is not past power, nor you past cure.
KING Art thou so confident? Within what space   155
        Hop'st thou my cure?
HELENA   The greatest grace lending grace,
        Ere twice the horses of the sun shall bring
        Their fiery torcher his diurnal ring,
        Ere twice in murk and occidental damp
        Moist Hesperus hath quenched her sleepy lamp,   160
        Or four and twenty times the pilot's glass
        Hath told the thievish minutes how they pass,
        What is infirm from your sound parts shall fly,
        Health shall live free, and sickness freely die.

Helena offers to risk her reputation and her life if she fails to cure the King.
If she succeeds, she asks for her choice of husband. The King agrees.

---

1 Helena's confidence (in pairs)

Helena risks more than just her life. Make a list of all the things that she puts at stake in lines 166–70 if she fails to cure the King. Then talk together about how you would want her to say lines 166–70. Should she sound 'monstrous desperate' (line 180), or just the opposite?

2 What convinces the King? (in pairs)

Read lines 171–82 carefully, and talk together about what it is that finally convinces the King to try Helena's cure.

3 'What do you promise me?' (in small groups)

It is not difficult to guess what Helena will choose as her reward. There are many other stories which depend on the main character undertaking some apparently impossible task to win something they desire. These stories are of different types: fairy-tales, like *Puss in Boots*, or the Russian version of Cinderella; myths, for example *Jason and the Argonauts*; or stories in the Romance tradition, such as Chaucer's *The Clerk's Tale*. Talk together about the advantages and disadvantages of using a familiar story pattern.

4 'By my sceptre and my hopes of help'

No one is quite sure whether Shakespeare wrote 'help' or 'heaven' in line 188. What do you think? Justify your choice to the rest of the class.

---

venter risk
Tax of impudence charge of
  shamelessness
strumpet prostitute
Traduced slandered
Seared branded (prostitutes were
  traditionally branded on the
  forehead)

Thou . . . hazard for you to risk
  this
monstrous desperate (that you
  are) utterly reckless
flinch in property fall short in
  respect
branch . . . state person of the
  royal family

KING Upon thy certainty and confidence   165
   What dar'st thou venter?
HELENA   Tax of impudence,
   A strumpet's boldness, a divulgèd shame,
   Traduced by odious ballads; my maiden's name
   Seared otherwise; ne worse of worst – extended
   With vilest torture, let my life be ended.   170
KING Methinks in thee some blessed spirit doth speak
   His powerful sound within an organ weak;
   And what impossibility would slay
   In common sense, sense saves another way.
   Thy life is dear, for all that life can rate   175
   Worth name of life in thee hath estimate:
   Youth, beauty, wisdom, courage, all
   That happiness and prime can happy call.
   Thou this to hazard needs must intimate
   Skill infinite, or monstrous desperate.   180
   Sweet practiser, thy physic I will try,
   That ministers thine own death if I die.
HELENA If I break time, or flinch in property
   Of what I spoke, unpitied let me die,
   And well deserved. Not helping, death's my fee,   185
   But if I help, what do you promise me?
KING Make thy demand.
HELENA   But will you make it even?
KING Ay, by my sceptre and my hopes of help.
HELENA Then shalt thou give me with thy kingly hand
   What husband in thy power I will command.   190
   Exempted be from me the arrogance
   To choose from forth the royal blood of France,
   My low and humble name to propagate
   With any branch or image of thy state;
   But such a one thy vassal, whom I know   195
   Is free for me to ask, thee to bestow.
KING Here is my hand, the premises observed,
   Thy will by my performance shall be served.
   So make the choice of thy own time, for I,
   Thy resolved patient, on thee still rely.   200

The King leads Helena away to question her further. In Scene 2, Lavatch jokes with the Countess about the manners required at court. He claims to have an answer for everything.

1 A sick joke? (in pairs)

One actor who played Lavatch suggested that lines 7–9 are an extreme example of black comedy. The actor imagines a 'lipless, handless, legless person' who truly would not be 'for the court'. Talk together about which present-day actors or comedians you think use a similar kind of humour. Which one of them do you think would make a fitting Lavatch?

2 'Highly fed and lowly taught' (in pairs)

Line 3 is from a proverb, 'better fed than taught', and shows Lavatch's opinion of the courtiers. All the references to social class so far have been about how impossible it is to rise in status. Talk together about how Lavatch overturns traditional ideas about class. Does Lavatch fit your idea of an alternative comedian?

3 A belly laugh

In lines 16–21 almost all Lavatch's examples of things which fit together are obscene. (A 'French crown' is a punk's or prostitute's fee, but can also mean 'syphilis'; 'Tib's rush' is a reference to rings made of rushes which were used in rustic mock-marriages, and also slang for 'vagina'.)

---

put ... height make a thorough test
breeding upbringing
put off dismiss
make a leg bow
pin thin
quatch plump

brawn fleshy
groat four pence
taffety punk prostitute dressed in taffeta
scolding quean nagging slut
pudding sausage

More should I question thee, and more I must –
Though more to know could not be more to trust –
From whence thou cam'st, how tended on, but rest
Unquestioned welcome and undoubted blest. –
Give me some help here ho! – If thou proceed   205
As high as word, my deed shall match thy deed.

Flourish. Exeunt

ACT 2 SCENE 2
The Palace of Rossillion

Enter the COUNTESS *and* LAVATCH

COUNTESS Come on, sir, I shall now put you to the height of your breeding.

LAVATCH I will show myself highly fed and lowly taught. I know my business is but to the court.

COUNTESS To the court! Why, what place make you special, when you   5
put off that with such contempt? But to the court!

LAVATCH Truly, madam, if God have lent a man any manners, he may easily put it off at court. He that cannot make a leg, put off's cap, kiss his hand, and say nothing, has neither leg, hands, lip, nor cap; and indeed such a fellow, to say precisely, were not for the court;   10
but for me, I have an answer will serve all men.

COUNTESS Marry, that's a bountiful answer that fits all questions.

LAVATCH It is like a barber's chair that fits all buttocks: the pin-buttock, the quatch-buttock, the brawn-buttock, or any buttock.

COUNTESS Will your answer serve fit to all questions?   15

LAVATCH As fit as ten groats is for the hand of an attorney, as your French crown for your taffety punk, as Tib's rush for Tom's forefinger, as a pancake for Shrove Tuesday, a morris for May-day, as the nail to his hole, the cuckold to his horn, as a scolding quean to a wrangling knave, as the nun's lip to the friar's mouth, nay, as   20
the pudding to his skin.

COUNTESS Have you, I say, an answer of such fitness for all questions?

Lavatch demonstrates his 'answer to fit all questions'. The Countess makes sure he understands that he must carry a letter to Helena and good wishes to Bertram.

Would you make any use of Lavatch's opinion of courtiers in the advice you give your actors and the way in which you costume them? Do you think that the designers of this production have considered Lavatch's views?

1 'O Lord, sir!' (in pairs)

Lavatch mocks the affected manners of courtiers with his all-purpose 'O Lord, sir!' reply. *Either* devise and present to the class a humorous routine of question and answer using lines 30–49 as your model, *or* use the actual lines and present them to the class making the scene as funny as possible.

putting off evasion
Thick quickly
homely meat plain food
is very sequent to will follow
closely (because it's a plea for mercy)

present immediate
Haste you again return home again

LAVATCH From below your duke to beneath your constable, it will fit
  any question.

COUNTESS It must be an answer of most monstrous size that must fit   25
  all demands.

LAVATCH But a trifle neither, in good faith, if the learned should speak
  truth of it. Here it is, and all that belongs to't. Ask me if I am a
  courtier: it shall do you no harm to learn.

COUNTESS To be young again, if we could! I will be a fool in question,   30
  hoping to be the wiser by your answer. I pray you, sir, are you a
  courtier?

LAVATCH O Lord, sir! – There's a simple putting off. More, more, a
  hundred of them.

COUNTESS Sir, I am a poor friend of yours that loves you.   35

LAVATCH O Lord, sir! – Thick, thick, spare not me.

COUNTESS I think, sir, you can eat none of this homely meat.

LAVATCH O Lord, sir! – Nay, put me to't, I warrant you.

COUNTESS You were lately whipped, sir, as I think.

LAVATCH O Lord, sir! – Spare not me.   40

COUNTESS Do you cry, 'O Lord, sir!' at your whipping, and 'Spare
  not me'? Indeed your 'O Lord, sir!' is very sequent to your
  whipping; you would answer very well to a whipping, if you were
  but bound to't.

LAVATCH I ne'er had worse luck in my life in my 'O Lord, sir!' I see   45
  things may serve long, but not serve ever.

COUNTESS I play the noble housewife with the time,
    To entertain it so merrily with a fool.

LAVATCH O Lord, sir! – Why, there't serves well again.

COUNTESS An end, sir; to your business: give Helen this,   50
    And urge her to a present answer back.
    Commend me to my kinsmen and my son.
  This is not much.

LAVATCH Not much commendation to them.

COUNTESS Not much employment for you. You understand me?   55

LAVATCH Most fruitfully. I am there before my legs.

COUNTESS Haste you again.

                                        Exeunt

Lafew and Bertram discuss the miraculous cure of the King. Their conversation is frequently interrupted by Parolles.

---

1 'So I say . . .' (in pairs)

In the BBC production's version of this episode, Lafew and Bertram are with other courtiers, and Parolles is constantly trying to edge into the conversation.

Improvise a scene in which one of you continually finishes the other's sentences. Choose a situation to suit your improvisation, for example: an absent-minded professor and a student, or an impatient parent with a young child. How does your improvisation help your reading of this scene?

2 Enter BERTRAM, LAFEW and PAROLLES (in groups of three)

Act out lines 1–34. Talk beforehand about what you want the audience to understand about the characters and the relationships between them.

3 Spread the news

Lafew is probably reading from a news-sheet or ballad reporting the King's miraculous cure. Ballad-sheets were narrative poems telling a political or sensational story. News-sheets and ballads were extremely popular and, like today's newspapers, did not always say what pleased those in power. In *The Winter's Tale* you can find exaggerated examples used by Autolycus to fool gullible peasants.

Write your version of the ballad-sheet which Lafew is reading. Use line 22 to start.

---

modern commonplace
causeless inexplicable
ensconcing sheltering
shot out (like a comet)
relinquished of abandoned by
Galen and Paracelsus old and new ways of treating disease

authentic fellows qualified doctors
actor agent
dolphin (the symbol of young love)
facinerious wicked
debile minister ineffectual agent

Paris The King's palace

Enter BERTRAM, LAFEW and PAROLLES

LAFEW They say miracles are past, and we have our philosophical persons, to make modern and familiar, things supernatural and causeless. Hence is it that we make trifles of terrors, ensconcing ourselves into seeming knowledge, when we should submit ourselves to an unknown fear. 5

PAROLLES Why, 'tis the rarest argument of wonder that hath shot out in our latter times.

BERTRAM And so 'tis.

LAFEW To be relinquished of the artists –

PAROLLES So I say, both of Galen and Paracelsus. 10

LAFEW Of all the learned and authentic fellows –

PAROLLES Right, so I say.

LAFEW That gave him out incurable –

PAROLLES Why, there 'tis, so say I too.

LAFEW Not to be helped – 15

PAROLLES Right, as 'twere a man assured of a –

LAFEW Uncertain life, and sure death.

PAROLLES Just, you say well; so would I have said.

LAFEW I may truly say it is a novelty to the world.

PAROLLES It is indeed; if you will have it in showing, you will read 20
it in what-do-ye-call there.

LAFEW [*Reading*] 'A showing of a heavenly effect in an earthly actor'.

PAROLLES That's it I would have said, the very same.

LAFEW Why, your dolphin is not lustier. 'Fore me, I speak in respect –

PAROLLES Nay, 'tis strange, 'tis very strange, that is the brief and the 25
tedious of it, and he's of a most facinerious spirit that will not acknowledge it to be the –

LAFEW Very hand of heaven.

PAROLLES Ay, so I say.

LAFEW In a most weak – 30

PAROLLES And debile minister, great power, great transcendence, which should indeed give us a further use to be made than alone the recovery of the king, as to be –

LAFEW Generally thankful.

*The King sits Helena by his side and praises her for her skill. He offers her
the choice of all the young men at court as a husband. Lafew wishes he were
young again.*

1 Costume change?

... And she comes in with the King, wearing a ball-dress that is just a
dream – her dream come true.

Sophie Thompson

(Helena in the 1992 Royal Shakespeare Company production)

Some productions make no change in Helena's costume in this scene
from the dark mourning dress she has been wearing in memory of her
father. Do you think a costume change here is appropriate, and if so,
what kind?

Lustique randy
tooth sweet tooth (for girls)
coranto lively dance
Mor du vinager! mock French
  oath (Parolles showing off?)
stand at my bestowing are my
  wards (I can give them in marriage)

frank election free choice
forsake refuse
bay curtal and his furniture bay
  horse and trappings
My . . . broken if I still had all my
  teeth (if I still were sexually active)

Enter KING, HELENA, *and* ATTENDANTS

PAROLLES I would have said it; you say well. Here comes the king.   35
LAFEW *Lustique*, as the Dutchman says; I'll like a maid the better whilst
    I have a tooth in my head. Why, he's able to lead her a coranto.
PAROLLES *Mor du vinager!* is not this Helen?
LAFEW 'Fore God, I think so.
KING Go call before me all the lords in court.   40
    Sit, my preserver, by thy patient's side,
    And with this healthful hand, whose banished sense
    Thou hast repealed, a second time receive
    The confirmation of my promised gift,
    Which but attends thy naming.   45

Enter three or four LORDS

    Fair maid, send forth thine eye. This youthful parcel
    Of noble bachelors stand at my bestowing,
    O'er whom both sovereign power and father's voice
    I have to use. Thy frank election make;
    Thou hast power to choose, and they none to forsake.   50
HELENA To each of you one fair and virtuous mistress
    Fall, when Love please! Marry, to each but one!
LAFEW I'd give bay curtal and his furniture,
    My mouth no more were broken than these boys',
    And writ as little beard.
KING   Peruse them well.   55
    Not one of those but had a noble father.
HELENA (*She addresses her to a Lord*) Gentlemen,
    Heaven hath through me restored the king to health.
ALL We understand it, and thank heaven for you.
HELENA I am a simple maid, and therein wealthiest   60
    That I protest I simply am a maid.
    Please it your majesty, I have done already.
    The blushes in my cheeks thus whisper me,
    'We blush that thou shouldst choose; but be refused,
    Let the white death sit on thy cheek for ever,   65
    We'll never come there again.'
KING   Make choice and see,
    Who shuns thy love shuns all his love in me.

Helena considers and rejects four lords. Lafew comments on the proceedings, but thinks that the lords are rejecting Helena. She finally chooses Bertram, who refuses to marry her.

1 Directing the choice (in groups of eight to ten)

a How you would help the actors playing the young lords to make their characters seem different?

b Talk together about how you would organise the movements for lines 69–96.
Either try it as a dance, *or* with the lords formally lined up, *or* with each of them moving one by one to Helena. Then try miming it. Where would you place Lafew (the pictures on page 79 will help you)?

c Bertram has not spoken since line 8. How would you direct him to behave?

d Act out some of your suggestions for **a–c** above, then assess which you think would be the most effective in performance.

2 Lafew's tone (in pairs)

Lafew's comments make it clear that he cannot hear what is being said by Helena and the lords. Try as many ways as you can of saying his lines, for example: ironically, angrily, sourly, or . . .?

Notice that English men had a reputation for being cold-hearted lovers even in the seventeenth century. What do you think Lafew expects Bertram to do (lines 92–3)?

Dian Diana (see page 94)
ames-ace two aces (Lafew means he would rather play this game than Russian roulette)
threat'ningly (the threat is that he wishes to accept her)
th'Turk . . . of the Turks had a reputation for castrating Christians

grape choice of the bunch
thy father drunk wine your father gave you good blood (proverb: good wine makes good blood)
I have . . . already I know what you are like

HELENA Now, Dian, from thy altar do I fly,
    And to imperial Love, that god most high,
    Do my sighs stream. [*To a first Lord*] Sir, will you hear my   70
      suit?
FIRST LORD And grant it.
HELENA   Thanks, sir; all the rest is mute.
LAFEW I had rather be in this choice than throw ames-ace for my life.
HELENA [*To a second Lord*] The honour, sir, that flames in your fair
      eyes,
    Before I speak, too threat'ningly replies.
    Love make your fortunes twenty times above   75
    Her that so wishes, and her humble love!
SECOND LORD No better, if you please.
HELENA   My wish receive,
    Which great love grant, and so I take my leave.
LAFEW Do all they deny her? And they were sons of mine, I'd have
    them whipped, or I would send them to th'Turk to make eunuchs   80
    of.
HELENA [*To a third Lord*] Be not afraid that I your hand should take,
    I'll never do you wrong for your own sake.
    Blessing upon your vows, and in your bed
    Find fairer fortune, if you ever wed!   85
LAFEW These boys are boys of ice, they'll none have her. Sure they are
    bastards to the English, the French ne'er got 'em.
HELENA [*To a fourth Lord*] You are too young, too happy, and too good,
    To make yourself a son out of my blood.
FOURTH LORD Fair one, I think not so.   90
LAFEW There's one grape yet; I am sure thy father drunk wine – but
    if thou be'st not an ass, I am a youth of fourteen. I have known
    thee already.
HELENA [*To Bertram*] I dare not say I take you, but I give
    Me and my service, ever whilst I live,   95
    Into your guiding power. – This is the man.
KING Why then, young Bertram, take her, she's thy wife.
BERTRAM My wife, my liege? I shall beseech your highness,
    In such a business, give me leave to use
    The help of mine own eyes.

> *Bertram says he cannot marry Helena because she is of inferior social class.*
> *The King criticises such a narrow view of honour. He says he will give*
> *Helena wealth and a title. Bertram again refuses Helena.*

1 What is honour? (in pairs)

The sense of what the King says in lines 109–36 is not new. Chaucer's Loathly Lady said much the same thing in *The Wife of Bath's Tale*: '... he is gentil that dooth gentil dedis' (true nobility comes from noble actions). The really radical thing about these lines is that they are spoken by a king who believes in a God-given hierarchy. Yet here he is saying that honour comes from honourable deeds, not from noble ancestors.

Go through lines 109–36 with your partner, dividing them into the separate arguments which the King uses to try to persuade Bertram that Helena's virtue makes her noble, in spite of her inferior status.

2 'I cannot love her' (in small groups)

So far in the play, the idea of the marriage has been presented from Helena's point of view, and Bertram's response is quite a shock. In fact, he does not speak to her at all; his lines are addressed to the King. How would you have Bertram address the King? He is, after all, a courtier. Is he peevish, pleading, stubborn, heart-broken . . .?

3 Sleeping Beauty turns down prince! (in pairs)

In most fairy-tales the gender role is reversed, with the hero/prince performing a magical deed and winning the goose-girl/princess. Bertram's reaction to Helena is as shocking as Sleeping Beauty refusing to marry the prince. Talk about how you think Helena feels at this moment.

Disdain . . . ever! let my rejection of her ruin my fortunes for ever
title (line 109) lack of title
Would . . . distinction could not be told apart
stands off . . . mighty title (social class) is held to be important
additions swell's noble titles make us great
dropsied unhealthily swollen
foregoers ancestors
lying trophy false epitaph
dower dowry
strive attempt

KING   Know'st thou not, Bertram,   100
    What she has done for me?
BERTRAM   Yes, my good lord,
    But never hope to know why I should marry her.
KING Thou know'st she has raised me from my sickly bed.
BERTRAM But follows it, my lord, to bring me down
    Must answer for your raising? I know her well;   105
    She had her breeding at my father's charge –
    A poor physician's daughter my wife? Disdain
    Rather corrupt me ever!
KING 'Tis only title thou disdain'st in her, the which
    I can build up. Strange is it that our bloods,   110
    Of colour, weight, and heat, poured all together,
    Would quite confound distinction, yet stands off
    In differences so mighty. If she be
    All that is virtuous – save what thou dislik'st,
    A poor physician's daughter – thou dislik'st   115
    Of virtue for the name. But do not so.
    From lowest place, whence virtuous things proceed,
    The place is dignified by th'doer's deed.
    Where great additions swell's, and virtue none,
    It is a dropsied honour. Good alone   120
    Is good, without a name; vileness is so:
    The property by what it is should go,
    Not by the title. She is young, wise, fair,
    In these to nature she's immediate heir;
    And these breed honour. That is honour's scorn   125
    Which challenges itself as honour's born
    And is not like the sire. Honours thrive,
    When rather from our acts we them derive
    Than our foregoers. The mere word's a slave
    Debauched on every tomb, on every grave   130
    A lying trophy, and as oft is dumb
    Where dust and damned oblivion is the tomb
    Of honoured bones indeed. What should be said?
    If thou canst like this creature as a maid,
    I can create the rest. Virtue and she   135
    Is her own dower; honour and wealth from me.
BERTRAM I cannot love her, nor will strive to do't.

The King says that his honour is questioned, and he threatens Bertram, who agrees to accept Helena. The King orders that the wedding should take place immediately.

1 The power of the King (in small groups)

Helena has said that she is willing to waive her reward (lines 139–40), but Bertram's refusal to obey the King is public defiance. Royal power is now the issue.

a One person reads lines 141–58 aloud slowly, while the rest echo all the words which are to do with power.

b The King's lines 141–58 are full of imagery. Look for imagery derived from:
bear-baiting 'my honour's at the stake'
imprisonment 'shackle up my love and her desert'
scales 'weigh thee to the beam'
gardening 'plant thine honour'
hunting 'both my revenge and hate loosing upon thee'.

2 I take her hand (in groups of eight to ten)

This is a key moment in the play: a visual symbol of the joining of Helena and Bertram. With one person as director, make a tableau of the court at line 168. The director then asks each actor to voice their thoughts about Bertram's action.

3 Tonight's the night!

The King insists (lines 169–75) that the marriage ceremony should be performed immediately, but the usual feast which should accompany it will have to wait for 'absent friends'. Why the haste?

---

strive to choose choose for yourself
misprision mistake
desert deserving
poising . . . scale adding my weight to her lightness (by giving her a title)
weigh . . . beam outweigh you

travails in works for
staggers . . . lapse giddiness and recklessness
dole quantity
replete abundant
else, does err otherwise you are a traitor

KING Thou wrong'st thyself, if thou shouldst strive to choose.
HELENA That you are well restored, my lord, I'm glad.
    Let the rest go.   140
KING My honour's at the stake, which to defeat,
    I must produce my power. Here, take her hand,
    Proud scornful boy, unworthy this good gift,
    That dost in vile misprision shackle up
    My love and her desert; that canst not dream,   145
    We poising us in her defective scale,
    Shall weigh thee to the beam; that wilt not know
    It is in us to plant thine honour where
    We please to have it grow. Check thy contempt;
    Obey our will, which travails in thy good;   150
    Believe not thy disdain, but presently
    Do thine own fortunes that obedient right
    Which both thy duty owes and our power claims;
    Or I will throw thee from my care for ever
    Into the staggers and the careless lapse   155
    Of youth and ignorance, both my revenge and hate
    Loosing upon thee, in the name of justice,
    Without all terms of pity. Speak, thine answer.
BERTRAM Pardon, my gracious lord; for I submit
    My fancy to your eyes. When I consider   160
    What great creation and what dole of honour
    Flies where you bid it, I find that she, which late
    Was in my nobler thoughts most base, is now
    The praisèd of the king, who so ennobled,
    Is as 'twere born so.
KING   Take her by the hand,   165
    And tell her she is thine; to whom I promise
    A counterpoise – if not to thy estate,
    A balance more replete.
BERTRAM   I take her hand.
KING Good fortune and the favour of the king
    Smile upon this contràct, whose ceremony   170
    Shall seem expedient on the now-born brief,
    And be performed tonight. The solemn feast
    Shall more attend upon the coming space,
    Expecting absent friends. As thou lov'st her,
    Thy love's to me religious; else, does err.   175
                                  Exeunt

Lafew tells Parolles that Bertram was wise to agree to marry Helena. Parolles takes offence at Lafew's language, but Lafew continues to insult Parolles and call him a coward.

1 What's it all about? (in pairs)

Talk together about what you think has caused the original quarrel between Lord Lafew and Parolles. Present your idea to the rest of the class, *either* as a mime, *or* by having each character tell his (different) side of the story.

2 Parolles' appearance

Lafew claims that it was Parolles' clothes that first made him suspicious about his character. He says that Parolles wears too many 'scarfs and . . . bannerets'. These were scarves, ribbons and badges often worn by soldiers, but Parolles overdoes it. Lafew keeps alluding to Parolles' appearance in his images, for example:

hen coward
casement window
bondage the scarves and military ribbons wrapped round him.

Do you still judge people by their clothes? For example, do you think you can tell someone's taste in music from the way they dress?

3 'He is a man I know'

Throughout the script opposite Lafew puns on the word 'man', which can mean either 'gentleman' or 'servant', depending on the context. Parolles is claiming to be equal to all gentlemen at line 184, but Lafew calls him 'count's man' (servant) in line 185. Which meaning do you think he has in mind at line 211?

How many times does Lafew remark he has 'found' (found out) or can see through, Parolles? As you read on, notice how often a similar phrase is used about Parolles.

succeeding consequences
to what is man to all men
of another style another thing altogether
write call myself a
ordinaries meal-times

make tolerable vent tell reasonable tales
pull . . . contrary swallow your foolishness to become wise
hold continue (or, ironically, 'discontinue')

Lafew and Parolles stay behind, commenting of this wedding

LAFEW Do you hear, monsieur? A word with you.

PAROLLES Your pleasure, sir?

LAFEW Your lord and master did well to make his recantation.

PAROLLES Recantation? My lord? My master?

LAFEW Ay; is it not a language I speak?   180

PAROLLES A most harsh one, and not to be understood without bloody
  succeeding. My master?

LAFEW Are you companion to the Count Rossillion?

PAROLLES To any count, to all counts: to what is man.

LAFEW To what is count's man. Count's master is of another style.   185

PAROLLES You are too old, sir; let it satisfy you, you are too old.

LAFEW I must tell thee, sirrah, I write man; to which title age cannot
  bring thee.

PAROLLES What I dare too well do, I dare not do.

LAFEW I did think thee, for two ordinaries, to be a pretty wise fellow. 190
  Thou didst make tolerable vent of thy travel; it might pass: yet the
  scarfs and the bannerets about thee did manifoldly dissuade me
  from believing thee a vessel of too great a burden. I have now found
  thee. When I lose thee again, I care not; yet art thou good for
  nothing but taking up, and that thou'rt scarce worth.   195

PAROLLES Hadst thou not the privilege of antiquity upon thee –

LAFEW Do not plunge thyself too far in anger, lest thou hasten thy trial;
  which if – Lord have mercy on thee for a hen! So, my good window
  of lattice, fare thee well. Thy casement I need not open, for I look
  through thee. Give me thy hand.   200

PAROLLES My lord, you give me most egregious indignity.

LAFEW Ay, with all my heart, and thou art worthy of it.

PAROLLES I have not, my lord, deserved it.

LAFEW Yes, good faith, every dram of it, and I will not bate thee a
  scruple.   205

PAROLLES Well, I shall be wiser.

LAFEW Even as soon as thou canst, for thou hast to pull at a smack
  a'th'contrary. If ever thou be'st bound in thy scarf and beaten, thou
  shalt find what it is to be proud of thy bondage. I have a desire
  to hold my acquaintance with thee, or rather my knowledge, that   210
  I may say in the default, 'He is a man I know.'

PAROLLES My lord, you do me most insupportable vexation.

*After Lafew has left, Parolles swears he will beat him if he sees him again.
Lafew returns, insults Parolles again and leaves. Bertram enters, depressed
about his marriage.*

1 'I'll beat him . . .' (in pairs)

Lafew's insults in lines 213–15 are puns on 'doing' and 'past'. 'Doing'
means 'action' or 'sexual intercourse', so Lafew means that he is past
taking action to beat Parolles, but he also has a little joke at his own
expense about being past sex. Notice that Parolles only dares to insult
Lafew after he has gone.

a Read lines 213–41 in role, then talk together about Lafew's insults.
Improvise the situation, using your own words, as energetically as
you can. Then play the situation again using Shakespeare's words,
retaining the energy of your improvisation – especially after the
re-entry of Lafew.

b Read lines 229–41 carefully, identifying what exactly Lafew
criticises about Parolles.

2 The insult circle (in groups of eight to ten)

Identify all the insults Lafew uses to Parolles in lines 197–241. (You
could also use those spoken by Helena in Act 1 Scene 1, or make up
others which seem appropriate.) Stand in a circle with one person as
Parolles in the centre and shout the insults at him.

Take turns at being in the centre. It is an unpleasant experience.
How can you make it comical?

3 'Let it be concealed awhile' (in pairs)

Explain what you think Parolles means by lines 242–3, and decide
what opinion you think he has of himself.

---

my poor doing my inadequate
power to make you suffer
as I will by thee just as I intend to
be past you
motion . . . leave as fast as my age
will let me
Sirrah sir (to a servant or child)
reservation reduction

hose stockings
lower part penis
breathe exercise (by beating)
picking . . . pomegranate a trivial
offence
commission warrant
heraldry coat of arms (right to call
yourself a gentleman)

LAFEW I would it were hell-pains for thy sake, and my poor doing
eternal; for doing I am past, as I will by thee, in what motion age
will give me leave.   *Exit* 215

PAROLLES Well, thou hast a son shall take this disgrace off me, scurvy,
old, filthy, scurvy lord! Well, I must be patient, there is no fettering
of authority. I'll beat him, by my life, if I can meet him with any
convenience, and he were double and double a lord. I'll have no
more pity of his age than I would have of – I'll beat him, and if 220
I could but meet him again.

Enter LAFEW

LAFEW Sirrah, your lord and master's married, there's news for you.
You have a new mistress.

PAROLLES I most unfeignedly beseech your lordship to make some
reservation of your wrongs. He is my good lord; whom I serve above 225
is my master.

LAFEW Who? God?

PAROLLES Ay, sir.

LAFEW The devil it is that's thy master. Why dost thou garter up thy
arms a'this fashion? Dost make hose of thy sleeves? Do other 230
servants so? Thou wert best set thy lower part where thy nose
stands. By mine honour, if I were but two hours younger, I'd beat
thee. Methink'st thou art a general offence, and every man should
beat thee. I think thou wast created for men to breathe themselves
upon thee.   235

PAROLLES This is hard and undeserved measure, my lord.

LAFEW Go to, sir, you were beaten in Italy for picking a kernel out of
a pomegranate. You are a vagabond and no true traveller. You are
more saucy with lords and honourable personages than the
commission of your birth and virtue gives you heraldry. You are 240
not worth another word, else I'd call you knave. I leave you. *Exit*

Enter [BERTRAM] *Count Rossillion*

PAROLLES Good, very good, it is so then. Good, very good, let it be
concealed awhile.

BERTRAM Undone, and forfeited to cares for ever!

PAROLLES What's the matter, sweet heart?   245

BERTRAM Although before the solemn priest I have sworn,
    I will not bed her.

Bertram tells Parolles that he has married Helena but will never sleep with her. Parolles persuades him to run away to the Italian wars. Bertram decides to send Helena home to Rossillion.

---

1 'I'll to the Tuscan wars, and never bed her' (in small groups)

In line 250, Bertram says for the second time that he will not sleep with Helena. Talk together about why you think this is so important to him.

Parolles seems just as keen to get away. What do you think are his reasons?

2 Honour? (in pairs)

Parolles' language is very coarse lines in 256–62. For example:

in a box unseen hiding his light under a bushel *or* female genitalia
manly marrow masculine courage *or* semen.

No one is quite sure what a 'kicky-wicky' is, but it's not hard to guess what Parolles probably has in mind. How would you advise the actor playing Parolles to say lines 274–7, and how would you describe the tone of Bertram's reply in lines 263–9?

3 Two letters

Bertram does not dare speak to the King, so he decides to write to him. And, without knowing what his mother will think of his marriage, he decides to write and tell her of his hatred of Helena. Write the two letters that he sends.

4 Shakespeare's autobiography? (in small groups)

Some people think that in line 269 Shakespeare is referring to his own wife, Anne Hathaway, left behind in Stratford-upon-Avon while he worked in London. Talk together about whether you think that is simply romantic fantasy.

---

curvet leap of a horse with all four legs off the ground at once
jades inferior horses (as opposed to Mars' fiery steed)
present gift money given as a wedding gift

furnish me to equip me for
caprichio whim
these balls bound now you're playing the game (of tennis); (why do you think Parolles uses this metaphor?)

PAROLLES What, what, sweet heart?

BERTRAM O my Parolles, they have married me!
    I'll to the Tuscan wars, and never bed her.   250

PAROLLES France is a dog-hole, and it no more merits
    The tread of a man's foot. To th'wars!

BERTRAM There's letters from my mother; what th'import is,
    I know not yet.

PAROLLES Ay, that would be known. To th'wars, my boy, to
    th'wars!   255
    He wears his honour in a box unseen,
    That hugs his kicky-wicky here at home,
    Spending his manly marrow in her arms,
    Which should sustain the bound and high curvet
    Of Mars's fiery steed. To other regions!   260
    France is a stable, we that dwell in't jades,
    Therefore to th'war!

BERTRAM It shall be so. I'll send her to my house,
    Acquaint my mother with my hate to her,
    And wherefore I am fled; write to the king   265
    That which I durst not speak. His present gift
    Shall furnish me to those Italian fields
    Where noble fellows strike. Wars is no strife
    To the dark house and the detested wife.

PAROLLES Will this caprichio hold in thee, art sure?   270

BERTRAM Go with me to my chamber, and advise me.
    I'll send her straight away. Tomorrow,
    I'll to the wars, she to her single sorrow.

PAROLLES Why, these balls bound, there's noise in it. 'Tis hard!
    A young man married is a man that's marred;   275
    Therefore away, and leave her bravely; go.
    The king has done you wrong; but hush, 'tis so.

                              Exeunt

Lavatch delivers the letter from the Countess to Helena, and jokes with her. Parolles comes in and Lavatch insults him.

---

1 Lavatch's fooling

Lavatch delivers to Helena the letter of Act 2 Scene 2. What can you deduce about the Countess's state of mind from Lavatch's words? (The obvious confusion of Lavatch's words probably reflects the Countess's feelings.)

2 'Why, I say nothing'

Parolles, like many people who talk too much, clearly thinks he is discreet. If you were going to play Parolles in a production of the play, what kind of preparation work would you do? Some actors choose an 'objective correlative' (someone they know with similar characteristics) as a model for their performance. Think of someone, or several people, on whom you can base your own portrayal of Parolles.

3 A 'witty fool' (in pairs)

Like Lord Lafew, Lavatch also says that he can see through Parolles. Read lines 14–28, taking roles as Lavatch and Parolles. Parolles has a higher social status than Lavatch, but notice how Lavatch undermines the conventional status relationship (see page 185). Try to bring this out in your reading. Look for other occasions in the play where Lavatch does this.

---

title status (and Parolles' name, meaning 'words')

Before me upon my soul (Lavatch also means that Parolles was a knave before him)

found thee found you out

in yourself by your own efforts (also, by looking at yourself)

ACT 2 SCENE 4
Paris   The King's palace

Enter HELENA *and* LAVATCH

HELENA My mother greets me kindly. Is she well?

LAVATCH She is not well, but yet she has her health. She's very merry, but yet she is not well; but thanks be given, she's very well, and wants nothing i'th'world; but yet she is not well.

HELENA If she be very well, what does she ail that she's not very well? 5

LAVATCH Truly, she's very well indeed, but for two things.

HELENA What two things?

LAVATCH One, that she's not in heaven, whither God send her quickly! the other, that she's in earth, from whence God send her quickly!

Enter PAROLLES

PAROLLES Bless you, my fortunate lady! 10

HELENA I hope, sir, I have your good will to have mine own good fortune.

PAROLLES You had my prayers to lead them on, and to keep them on, have them still. O, my knave, how does my old lady?

LAVATCH So that you had her wrinkles and I her money, I would she 15
did as you say.

PAROLLES Why, I say nothing.

LAVATCH Marry, you are the wiser man; for many a man's tongue shakes out his master's undoing. To say nothing, to do nothing, to know nothing, and to have nothing, is to be a great part of your 20
title, which is within a very little of nothing.

PAROLLES Away, th'art a knave.

LAVATCH You should have said, sir, 'Before a knave th'art a knave', that's 'Before me th'art a knave.' This had been truth, sir.

PAROLLES Go to, thou art a witty fool, I have found thee. 25

LAVATCH Did you find me in yourself, sir, or were you taught to find me? The search, sir, was profitable, and much fool may you find in you, even to the world's pleasure and the increase of laughter.

69

*Parolles gives Helena a message from Bertram. She is to make up an excuse
for taking leave of the King, then wait for further instructions from Bertram.
Bertram tells Lafew about Parolles' bravery.*

1 Parolles' sweet words

'Well fed' (line 29) is another reference to the proverb, 'better fed
than taught' which is an echo of an earlier line in Act 2 Scene 2. Look
back and see if you can find the line.

Because Parolles suddenly changes to verse, lines 29–38 seem like
a carefully prepared and rehearsed excuse for why Bertram will not
sleep with Helena on their wedding night. Parolles is suggesting that
a delay will make the 'rite of love' sweeter when it does happen.

2 '. . . Your due time claims'

Under Church law, their marriage would not be valid until it had
been consummated (line 33). Bertram is legally bound to make love to
Helena to make the marriage binding.

3 Helena's response (in pairs)

Decide what you think of Helena's meek response to Parolles
(line 45). Do you think her words truly represent her feelings? Bear
this episode in mind during the next two occasions when Helena is
on-stage.

4 Directing the action (in groups of three)

What kind of stage business (activity) would you give your actors
during lines 1–11? Bertram and Lafew must be in the middle of a
conversation when they enter, because Lafew refers to 'he' without
defining who 'he' is. Take turns to direct this short episode and try to
give the actors something to do which is motivated by the script
(Bertram could be packing, shaving or writing letters).

---

your due time wedding night
sweets flowers
curbèd time time of waiting
valiant approof demonstrated
  courage
deliverance words

dial pocket watch
bunting a bird which resembles the
  lark, except for its singing
accordingly correspondingly
amity friendship

PAROLLES A good knave, i'faith, and well fed.
   Madam, my lord will go away tonight,   30
   A very serious business calls on him.
   The great prerogative and rite of love,
   Which, as your due time claims, he does acknowledge,
   But puts it off to a compelled restraint;
   Whose want, and whose delay, is strewed with sweets,   35
   Which they distill now in the curbèd time,
   To make the coming hour o'erflow with joy,
   And pleasure drown the brim.
HELENA   What's his will else?
PAROLLES That you will take your instant leave a'th'king,
   And make this haste as your own good proceeding,   40
   Strengthened with what apology you think
   May make it probable need.
HELENA   What more commands he?
PAROLLES That having this obtained, you presently
   Attend his further pleasure.
HELENA In every thing I wait upon his will.   45
PAROLLES I shall report it so.   *Exit Parolles*
HELENA   I pray you. Come, sirrah.
               Exeunt

ACT 2 SCENE 5
Paris The King's palace

Enter LAFEW and BERTRAM

LAFEW But I hope your lordship thinks not him a soldier.
BERTRAM Yes, my lord, and of very valiant approof.
LAFEW You have it from his own deliverance.
BERTRAM And by other warranted testimony.
LAFEW Then my dial goes not true. I took this lark for a bunting. 5
BERTRAM I do assure you, my lord, he is very great in knowledge, and
  accordingly valiant.
LAFEW I have then sinned against his experience, and transgressed
  against his valour, and my state that way is dangerous, since I cannot
  yet find in my heart to repent. Here he comes. I pray you make 10
  us friends, I will pursue the amity.

Parolles tells Bertram that Helena will do as he asks. Lafew insults Parolles again, and warns Bertram not to trust Parolles in any important matter.

1 Playing Lafew

Lafew cannot try to 'pursue the amity' once he is faced with Parolles again, and his first words are about Parolles' appearance. He makes fun of Parolles' shocked response to his question by pretending to take 'sir' to be the name of his tailor. 'Like him that leapt into the custard' (lines 32–3) is a reference to the famous tradition of a jester leaping into an enormous custard pie at the annual feast of the Lord Mayor of London.

a If you were playing Lafew, what would you do during lines 17–24 when Bertram and Parolles are having a conversation which you are not supposed to hear?

b By the time Lafew leaves the stage, he has made a very explicit warning to Bertram not to trust Parolles. If you were directing the scene, where would you want Lafew to change the tone of his advice?

2 'Here comes my clog' (in pairs)

A clog (line 47) was a wooden block tied to an animal's leg to prevent it straying too far. The sense of the word and the sound suggest Bertram's attitude to Helena. Many derogatory words have been applied to women over the centuries; comparatively few are used about men. One of the themes of the play is the unequal relationship between men and women (see page 181). Choose four words for Bertram which express your opinion of him.

---

casketed packed
something a form of entertainment
  (by telling amusing stories)
made shift managed
suffer . . . residence explain why
  you are there

at's at his
heavy important
of them tame creatures like
  Parolles as pets
idle foolish
worthy pass good reputation

Enter PAROLLES

PAROLLES [*To Bertram*] These things shall be done, sir.

LAFEW Pray you, sir, who's his tailor?

PAROLLES Sir!

LAFEW O, I know him well, I, sir, he, sir, 's a good workman, a very   15
good tailor.

BERTRAM [*Aside to Parolles*] Is she gone to the king?

PAROLLES She is.

BERTRAM Will she away tonight?

PAROLLES As you'll have her.   20

BERTRAM I have writ my letters, casketed my treasure,
　　　　Given order for our horses, and tonight,
　　　　When I should take possession of the bride,
　　　　End ere I do begin.

LAFEW A good traveller is something at the latter end of a dinner, but   25
one that lies three thirds, and uses a known truth to pass a thousand
nothings with, should be once heard and thrice beaten. God save
you, captain.

BERTRAM Is there any unkindness between my lord and you, monsieur?

PAROLLES I know not how I have deserved to run into my lord's   30
displeasure.

LAFEW You have made shift to run into't, boots and spurs and all, like
him that leapt into the custard; and out of it you'll run again, rather
than suffer question for your residence.

BERTRAM It may be you have mistaken him, my lord.   35

LAFEW And shall do so ever, though I took him at's prayers. Fare you
well, my lord, and believe this of me: there can be no kernel in this
light nut; the soul of this man is his clothes. Trust him not in matter
of heavy consequence; I have kept of them tame, and know their
natures. Farewell, monsieur, I have spoken better of you than you   40
have or will to deserve at my hand, but we must do good against
evil.   [*Exit*]

PAROLLES An idle lord, I swear.

BERTRAM I think so.

PAROLLES Why, do you not know him?   45

BERTRAM Yes, I do know him well, and common speech
　　　　Gives him a worthy pass. Here comes my clog.

Bertram tells Helena that she must go immediately to Rossillion and not question why he is neglecting his duties as a husband. He says he will follow her after two days.

1 Eye contact (in pairs)

One person plays Bertram and the other Helena. Read lines 48–71 with Helena looking directly at Bertram while he speaks. Bertram should make a definite pause at each full stop and meet Helena's eyes. What effect do the pauses have on the sound of Bertram's speech? Afterwards try reading lines 51–65 without pauses. Compare the two styles.

Choose a line from the script opposite as a caption for this picture.

present parting immediate departure
holds . . . time is not suitable for a wedding day
nor . . . particular and does not fulfil my duties as a husband

muse wonder
respects reasons
observance dutiful service
eke out compensate for

Enter HELENA

HELENA I have, sir, as I was commanded from you,
    Spoke with the king, and have procured his leave
    For present parting; only he desires   50
    Some private speech with you.
BERTRAM   I shall obey his will.
    You must not marvel, Helen, at my course,
    Which holds not colour with the time, nor does
    The ministration and requirèd office
    On my particular. Prepared I was not   55
    For such a business; therefore am I found
    So much unsettled. This drives me to entreat you,
    That presently you take your way for home,
    And rather muse than ask why I entreat you,
    For my respects are better than they seem,   60
    And my appointments have in them a need
    Greater than shows itself at the first view
    To you that know them not. This to my mother.
            [Giving a letter]
    'Twill be two days ere I shall see you, so
    I leave you to your wisdom.
HELENA   Sir, I can nothing say,   65
    But that I am your most obedient servant.
BERTRAM Come, come, no more of that.
HELENA   And ever shall
    With true observance seek to eke out that
    Wherein toward me my homely stars have failed
    To equal my great fortune.
BERTRAM   Let that go.   70
    My haste is very great. Farewell; hie home.

> *Helena hesitantly asks Bertram if he will kiss her because she is leaving.*
> *When she is gone, he tells Parolles that he will not go home but to*
> *the Italian wars.*

1 What does Helena want? (a whole class activity)

Bertram is clearly anxious for Helena to leave, and she is nervous
about asking for what she wants. If you have access to a large space,
spread out and work on your own without looking at anyone else.
Read Helena's lines 73–80 aloud, ignoring Bertram's reply. Walk
forward while you are reading, making a definite change of direction
at each punctuation mark. If you have to stay in your seat, work in
pairs, changing speaker at each punctuation mark. What does the
fragmentation of Helena's speeches (and the incomplete line 79) tell
you about her mood? How do you think Shakespeare is directing the
the actor here?

2 Do they kiss? (in groups of four)

How do Helena and Bertram part?

- Does he agree to her request and kiss her?
- Does he kiss her hand?
- Does he ignore her altogether?
- Are they close, or far apart?
- Do they speak loudly or quietly?
- Do they make eye contact, or avoid meeting each other's eyes?

Take it in turns for one pair to act out different ways of playing this
scene while the other pair watches and makes constructive comments.
If you think you have found a particularly successful way, show it to
the rest of the class.

---

owe own
fain willingly
vouch affirm to be

sunder part
corragio! courage!

HELENA Pray, sir, your pardon.
BERTRAM   Well, what would you say?
HELENA I am not worthy of the wealth I owe,
      Nor dare I say 'tis mine; and yet it is;
      But like a timorous thief, most fain would steal   75
      What law does vouch mine own.
BERTRAM   What would you have?
HELENA Something, and scarce so much; nothing indeed.
      I would not tell you what I would, my lord.
      Faith, yes:
      Strangers and foes do sunder, and not kiss.   80
BERTRAM I pray you stay not, but in haste to horse.
HELENA I shall not break your bidding, good my lord.
      Where are my other men? Monsieur, farewell.   *Exit*
BERTRAM Go thou toward home, where I will never come
      Whilst I can shake my sword or hear the drum.   85
      Away, and for our flight.
PAROLLES   Bravely, *corragio*!
                                     Exeunt

Looking back at Act 2
Activities for groups or individuals

1 Defying the King

At the time in which the play is set the power of the monarch was immense. To defy the King was almost unthinkable – it was compared to defying God. In *Sir Thomas More* (a play which some people think was partly written by Shakespeare), this belief is made explicit in one of More's speeches:

> . . . to the King God hath his office lent
> Of dread, of justice, power and command;
> Hath bid him rule, and willed you to obey.
> And to add ampler majesty to this
> He hath not only lent the king his figure,
> His throne and sword, but given him his own name;
> Calling him a God on earth. What do you then
> Rising 'gainst him that God himself installs
> But rise 'gainst God?

Talk together about how you would show Bertram's feelings during his defiance and his surrender.

2 A magical cure? (in pairs)

Read the conversation between Helena and the King in Scene 1 (lines 95–206). Make a note of every time there is a reference to some kind of supernatural power assisting Helena. Compare your evidence with another pair's.

3 The court

How would you present Scene 3? In the script, Helena is the only woman present. Would you want any other women there, as partners for the young lords, or perhaps attendants? Or would you want to emphasise Helena's vulnerability by leaving her unattended? Count how many lines Helena has in Scene 3 once she has chosen Bertram. What does this suggest about her status?

4 An arranged marriage

Traditionally, aristocratic marriages were arranged by parents for reasons of wealth and status, so that money stayed within the family. Today, arranged marriages are still common in many cultures. Draw up a list of the advantages and disadvantages of parents or guardians deciding who young people should marry.

Two versions of the 'choosing'. Which comes closest to your expectations of the scene?

The Duke of Florence expresses surprise that the King of France will not send troops to the Italian wars. The First Lord Dumaine suggests that many young French lords will volunteer to fight.

1 Polite excuses (in small groups)

The Second Lord Dumaine is in a difficult position. He tells the Duke he cannot supply ('yield') reasons why the French have not agreed to send troops to help the Florentines. He has not attended state council meetings and can only speculate about ('frame') what has happened ('the great figure'). His imagination is rather inadequate ('self-unable motion'). Compare his diplomatic reply to the Duke of Florence with the King's speech in Act 1 Scene 2, lines 11–15.

In lines 17–19, the First Lord Dumaine suggests
that war will be a cure for the young men who have overdosed on the 'ease'
of a life of peace. Do you think that is what this photograph suggests?

great decision violently decisive battles
shut his bosom hardened his heart
borrowing prayers pleas for help
surfeit on their ease are sickened by peace

physic to be cured (by bloodletting)
avails benefit
th'field the battlefield
Flourish trumpet fanfare

ACT 3 SCENE 1
Florence   The Duke's palace

Trumpet fanfare   Enter the DUKE OF FLORENCE, *the* FIRST *and*
SECOND LORDS *Dumaine and a troop of soldiers*

DUKE So that from point to point now have you heard
        The fundamental reasons of this war,
        Whose great decision hath much blood let forth
        And more thirsts after.

FIRST LORD   Holy seems the quarrel
        Upon your grace's part; black and fearful   5
        On the opposer.

DUKE Therefore we marvel much our cousin France
        Would in so just a business shut his bosom
        Against our borrowing prayers.

SECOND LORD   Good my lord,
        The reasons of our state I cannot yield   10
        But like a common and an outward man
        That the great figure of a council frames
        By self-unable motion, therefore dare not
        Say what I think of it, since I have found
        Myself in my incertain grounds to fail   15
        As often as I guessed.

DUKE   Be it his pleasure.

FIRST LORD But I am sure the younger of our nature,
        That surfeit on their ease, will day by day
        Come here for physic.

DUKE   Welcome shall they be;
        And all the honours that can fly from us   20
        Shall on them settle. – You know your places well;
        When better fall, for your avails they fell.
        Tomorrow to th'field.

                                   Flourish. [*Exeunt*]

Lavatch says Bertram is sad. He adds that he himself no longer has any interest in Isbel. The Countess reads Bertram's letter. It reveals that he has married Helena, but will not sleep with her.

1 Lavatch

Although described as a clown or fool, Lavatch is perceptive and quick-witted. He recognises the 'melancholy' in Bertram. His fortunes reflect Helena's: she wanted to marry Bertram, he wanted to marry Isbel. Now both relationships have soured. Bertram refuses to consummate his marriage, and Lavatch is becoming more interested in money than sex. The 'old ling' in his cod-piece is useless. Do you think he is really serious, or just joking?

2 Bertram – son and husband (in small groups)

a Bertram emphasises that he will not 'bed' Helena. His language sounds crude when used to Parolles. What do you think of Bertram using such language in a letter to his mother?

b Imagine Bertram reads the letter aloud to Parolles before sending it. Experiment with different ways of reading, for example: Do you think he is proud of his turn of phrase? (Note that he makes a pun on the knot of marriage in line 18.)

c 'Rash and unbridled boy' echoes the King's words in Act 2 Scene 3, line 143, emphasising Bertram's youth and the adults' opinions of him. Do you think these descriptions are simply an example of the generation gap, or does Bertram deserve such strong criticisms?

---

ruff a frill on a collar or boot
trick of melancholy streak of sadness in his personality
old ling sexual desire, penis
brains . . . out I have finished with my former love

stomach appetite
recovered cured
pluck bring down
misprising scorning
the contempt of empire even an emperor to despise her

ACT 3 SCENE 2
The Palace of Rossillion

Enter the COUNTESS *and* LAVATCH

COUNTESS It hath happened all as I would have had it, save that he
comes not along with her.

LAVATCH By my troth, I take my young lord to be a very melancholy
man.

COUNTESS By what observance, I pray you?   5

LAVATCH Why, he will look upon his boot and sing, mend the ruff and
sing, ask questions and sing, pick his teeth and sing. I know a man
that had this trick of melancholy sold a goodly manor for a song.

COUNTESS Let me see what he writes, and when he means to come.

[Opening the letter]

LAVATCH I have no mind to Isbel since I was at court. Our old lings   10
and our Isbels a'th'country are nothing like your old ling and your
Isbels a'th'court. The brains of my Cupid's knocked out, and I
begin to love, as an old man loves money, with no stomach.

COUNTESS What have we here?

LAVATCH E'en that you have there.   *Exit*   15

[COUNTESS] [*Reads*] *a letter* 'I have sent you a daughter-in-law; she
hath recovered the king, and undone me. I have wedded her, not
bedded her, and sworn to make the "not" eternal. You shall hear
I am run away; know it before the report come. If there be breadth
enough in the world, I will hold a long distance. My duty to you.   20
                          Your unfortunate son,
                                   Bertram.'

        This is not well, rash and unbridled boy,
        To fly the favours of so good a king,
        To pluck his indignation on thy head   25
        By the misprising of a maid too virtuous
        For the contempt of empire.

*Enter [*LAVATCH, *the] Clown*

LAVATCH O madam, yonder is heavy news within between two soldiers
and my young lady!

83

Lavatch tells the Countess that Bertram has run away. The Lords Dumaine confirm the news. Helena reads Bertram's letter. It sets her two apparently impossible tasks.

1 Sexual joking

Even when he hears the bad news about Bertram, Lavatch continues with his sexual puns ('standing to't' means staying at your post in battle, or having an erection). What do you think is the Countess's reaction? Perhaps she is so absorbed in her news that she is not even listening.

2 Impossible tasks (in pairs)

The fairy-tale seems to come to an abrupt end when Bertram rejects Helena. It is as if Prince Charming is rejecting Cinderella. Now the threads of a different fairy-tale are spun, in which the heroine is set an impossible task. Such tasks are a common feature of children's stories. In the fairy-tale *Rumpelstiltskin*, the main character has to discover the name of the little man who has helped her. If she cannot do so, she must give him her first child.

a Identify the two conditions which Helena must fulfil before Bertram will acknowledge her as his wife.

b Take parts as Helena and the Countess. Helena reads aloud Bertram's letter. The Countess must decide how to react to it.

---

quirks sudden changes
face appearance
on the start when it suddenly appears
woman me make me cry
dispatch in hand urgent business

bend return
If thou . . . moiety if you take all the miseries on you, you rob me of my share
good convenience claims he can reasonably claim

COUNTESS What is the matter?   30

LAVATCH Nay, there is some comfort in the news, some comfort. Your
son will not be killed so soon as I thought he would.

COUNTESS Why should he be killed?

LAVATCH So say I, madam, if he run away, as I hear he does. The
danger is in standing to't; that's the loss of men, though it be the   35
getting of children. Here they come will tell you more. For my part,
I only hear your son was run away.

Enter HELENA *and two Gentlemen* [*the* FIRST *and* SECOND LORDS
DUMAINE]

SECOND LORD 'Save you, good madam.

HELENA Madam, my lord is gone, for ever gone.

FIRST LORD Do not say so.   40

COUNTESS Think upon patience. Pray you, gentlemen,
    I have felt so many quirks of joy and grief
    That the first face of neither on the start
    Can woman me unto't. Where is my son, I pray you?

FIRST LORD Madam, he's gone to serve the Duke of Florence.   45
    We met him thitherward, for thence we came;
    And after some dispatch in hand at court,
    Thither we bend again.

HELENA Look on his letter, madam, here's my passport.
    [*Reads*] 'When thou canst get the ring upon my finger, which never   50
shall come off, and show me a child begotten of thy body that I
am father to, then call me husband; but in such a "then" I write
a "never".' This is a dreadful sentence.

COUNTESS Brought you this letter, gentlemen?

FIRST LORD Ay, madam, and for the contents' sake are sorry for our   55
pains.

COUNTESS I prithee, lady, have a better cheer;
    If thou engrossest all the griefs are thine,
    Thou robb'st me of a moiety. He was my son,
    But I do wash his name out of my blood,   60
    And thou art all my child. Towards Florence is he?

FIRST LORD Ay, madam.

COUNTESS   And to be a soldier?

FIRST LORD Such is his noble purpose, and believe't,
    The duke will lay upon him all the honour
    That good convenience claims.

Helena reads out another bitter remark from Bertram's letter. The Countess blames Parolles for corrupting Bertram's character. The Lords Dumaine agree with her opinion of Parolles.

1 I can't believe it!

Helena is clearly shocked by the letter she is holding. As director, what would you advise her to do while the Countess talks to the Lords Dumaine?

2 'Brought you this letter?' (in groups of four)

In Act 2 Scene 1, Bertram first met the Lords Dumaine and was encouraged by Parolles to make friends with them. They have now been persuaded by Bertram to bring painful news to his mother and his wife.

a Take parts and read lines 38–90. Decide how the two Lords now feel about Bertram. In their responses to the Countess, are they making excuses for Bertram out of embarrassment, or because they believe in what they are saying? Consider their reaction as Helena reads her letter.

b Divide into two pairs and improvise the conversation the Lords Dumaine have after leaving the Countess. Include their reaction to her message to Bertram: that no matter how honourably he fights on the battlefield, he cannot make up for his dishonourable behaviour towards Helena (lines 84–6).

'Till I have . . . nothing in France' while my wife lives in France, I have nothing worth returning for
haply perhaps
tainted corrupt
a well-derivèd nature his inherited good nature

his inducement Parolles' encouragement
that too much self-conceit
holds him much to have gives him an inflated opinion of himself
Not . . . courtesies you serve me only in so far as we exchange polite greetings

COUNTESS   Return you thither?   65
SECOND LORD Ay, madam, with the swiftest wing of speed.
HELENA [*Reads*] 'Till I have no wife, I have nothing in France.'
      'Tis bitter.
COUNTESS   Find you that there?
HELENA   Ay, madam.
SECOND LORD 'Tis but the boldness of his hand haply, which his heart
      was not consenting to.   70
COUNTESS Nothing in France, until he have no wife!
      There's nothing here that is too good for him
      But only she, and she deserves a lord
      That twenty such rude boys might tend upon,
      And call her hourly mistress. Who was with him?   75
SECOND LORD A servant only, and a gentleman
      Which I have sometime known.
COUNTESS   Parolles, was it not?
SECOND LORD Ay, my good lady, he.
COUNTESS A very tainted fellow, and full of wickedness.
      My son corrupts a well-derivèd nature   80
      With his inducement.
SECOND LORD   Indeed, good lady,
      The fellow has a deal of that too much,
      Which holds him much to have.
COUNTESS   Y'are welcome, gentlemen.
      I will entreat you, when you see my son,
      To tell him that his sword can never win   85
      The honour that he loses. More I'll entreat you
      Written to bear along.
FIRST LORD   We serve you, madam,
      In that and all your worthiest affairs.
COUNTESS Not so, but as we change our courtesies.
      Will you draw near?   90
                          Exit [with the Lords Dumaine]

Alone, Helena blames herself for the dangers Bertram will face in battle. She decides to leave France.

---

1 Voicing your thoughts (a whole class activity)

This is the third occasion on which Helena speaks a soliloquy. She seems appalled that her actions have led to Bertram's running away to war. Sophie Thompson (Helena in the Royal Shakespeare Company 1992 production) said she felt Helena was devastated that her love for Bertram might lead to his death. She therefore wept as she spoke the words. Choose one or more of the following to help you understand how Helena's mind is working:

a Walk while you read the soliloquy aloud, changing direction at each punctuation mark. Talk about how the turning movement helps to emphasise Helena's feelings and bring her to her final decision.

b Brainstorm your ideas about how an actor could deliver this soliloquy on-stage. For example, Helena could read the first line from the letter she is holding, and then speak the following lines to a portrait of Bertram.

c One person reads the soliloquy aloud, pausing after the phrases in which Helena speaks about herself. The others echo each phrase for emphasis, for example 'I set him there'. Alternatively choose one phrase such as 'I am the cause', and repeat it after every sentence.

d One person reads the soliloquy aloud. The others echo every word connected with war.

e Repeat exercise d, echoing words about Bertram. Consider why Helena twice calls him just 'Rossillion', and not 'my lord' or 'Bertram'.

---

event hazard
sportive lively
mark target
leaden messengers bullets
forward breast brave heart
caitiff despicable person

ravin ravenous
Whence . . . all from a war which may lead to an honourable scar, but just as often leads to loss of life
officed all did all the household duties

HELENA   'Till I have no wife, I have nothing in France.'
Nothing in France, until he has no wife!
Thou shalt have none, Rossillion, none in France;
Then hast thou all again. Poor lord, is't I
That chase thee from thy country, and expose   95
Those tender limbs of thine to the event
Of the none-sparing war? And is it I
That drive thee from the sportive court, where thou
Wast shot at with fair eyes, to be the mark
Of smoky muskets? O you leaden messengers,   100
That ride upon the violent speed of fire,
Fly with false aim, move the still-piercing air
That sings with piercing, do not touch my lord.
Whoever shoots at him, I set him there;
Whoever charges on his forward breast,   105
I am the caitiff that do hold him to't;
And though I kill him not, I am the cause
His death was so effected. Better 'twere
I met the ravin lion when he roared
With sharp constraint of hunger; better 'twere   110
That all the miseries which nature owes
Were mine at once. No, come thou home, Rossillion,
Whence honour but of danger wins a scar,
As oft it loses all. I will be gone.
My being here it is that holds thee hence.   115
Shall I stay here to do't? No, no, although
The air of paradise did fan the house,
And angels officed all. I will be gone,
That pitiful rumour may report my flight
To consolate thine ear. Come night, end day!   120
For with the dark, poor thief, I'll steal away.   *Exit*

The Duke of Florence appoints Bertram as a commander of his cavalry. Bertram swears to be a follower of Mars, the god of war, and to abandon love.

1 Bertram's rapid promotion

Bertram seems to be achieving military honour in Florence – a contrast with the way he has handled his personal life. The Duke mentions fortune twice in this scene. Perhaps he sees this young soldier as a good luck mascot. What do you think Bertram has done to gain such a quick promotion?

2 Spectacular? (in groups of four)

The stage directions suggest that this short scene is a grand spectacle. Talk together about different ways of staging the scene. If you were filming it, how would you exploit the opportunities for tracking or panning shots and a large cast of extras?

3 The family portrait gallery (in pairs)

Imagine that Bertram has his portrait painted for his mother. One of you acts as Bertram, the other as the artist. Using the final line of Scene 3 as your guide, put Bertram in a pose suitable for the painting. The 'artists' inspect the 'portraits'. What are the similarities and differences?

---

lay wager
credence belief
extreme edge of hazard utmost
  limit of danger

prosperous helm lucky helmet
file ranks

ACT 3 SCENE 3
Florence   Near the battlefield

Trumpet fanfare   Enter the DUKE OF FLORENCE, BERTRAM,
PAROLLES, *drummers and buglers, soldiers*

DUKE The general of our horse thou art, and we,
  Great in our hope, lay our best love and credence
  Upon thy promising fortune.
BERTRAM   Sir, it is
  A charge too heavy for my strength, but yet
  We'll strive to bear it for your worthy sake   5
  To th'extreme edge of hazard.
DUKE   Then go thou forth,
  And Fortune play upon thy prosperous helm
  As thy auspicious mistress!
BERTRAM   This very day,
  Great Mars, I put myself into thy file;
  Make me but like my thoughts, and I shall prove 10
  A lover of thy drum, hater of love.
                Exeunt

Rinaldo reads Helena's letter to the Countess. It reveals that Helena has left Rossillion to travel as a pilgrim. The Countess rebukes Rinaldo for allowing Helena to leave.

1 Helena's sonnet-letter (in pairs)

Helena's letter (lines 4–17) is written in the form of a sonnet. A sonnet is a poem of fourteen lines, with each line containing ten syllables. The Shakespearean sonnet has three sections:

- the first eight lines (rhyming ABABCDCD)
- the next four lines (rhyming EFEF)
- a rhyming couplet to end (GG) – this can either sum up the main idea of the whole poem or turn it upside down.

Shakespeare wrote a series of 154 sonnets and occasionally used sonnets in his plays. For example, in *Romeo and Juliet* there are three complete sonnets.

a Talk together about what you think are Helena's feelings, as expressed in lines 4–17. Choose a line or pair of lines which you consider to be the key to the whole letter. Compare your choice with the rest of the class. How many pairs have chosen the final couplet?

b Write your own sonnet, using the information above. Express in your sonnet *either* the Countess's thoughts at this point in the play *or* Helena's thoughts as she begins her journey.

Saint Jaques St James's shrine at Santiago de Compostella in Spain
hie hurry home
His taken labours the tasks he has undertaken
despiteful Juno the goddess Juno hated Hercules because he was the result of adultery by her husband Jupiter, king of the gods; she drove Hercules mad

dogs the heels of worth pursues brave men
lack advice show such poor judgement
overnight last evening

ACT 3 SCENE 4
The Palace of Rossillion

Enter the COUNTESS *and* RINALDO

COUNTESS Alas! and would you take the letter of her?
　　　Might you not know she would do as she has done
　　　By sending me a letter? Read it again.
[RINALDO] [*Reads*] *letter*
　　　'I am Saint Jaques' pilgrim, thither gone.
　　　Ambitious love hath so in me offended　　　　　　5
　　　That barefoot plod I the cold ground upon
　　　With sainted vow my faults to have amended.
　　　Write, write, that from the bloody course of war
　　　My dearest master, your dear son, may hie.
　　　Bless him at home in peace, whilst I from far　　10
　　　His name with zealous fervour sanctify.
　　　His taken labours bid him me forgive;
　　　I, his despiteful Juno, sent him forth
　　　From courtly friends, with camping foes to live,
　　　Where death and danger dogs the heels of worth.　15
　　　He is too good and fair for death and me,
　　　Whom I myself embrace to set him free.'
COUNTESS Ah, what sharp stings are in her mildest words!
　　　Rinaldo, you did never lack advice so much
　　　As letting her pass so. Had I spoke with her,　　20
　　　I could have well diverted her intents,
　　　Which thus she hath prevented.
RINALDO　　　　　　　　　　　Pardon me, madam,
　　　If I had given you this at overnight,
　　　She might have been o'erta'en; and yet she writes,
　　　Pursuit would be but vain.

The Countess instructs Rinaldo to write to Bertram to tell him of Helena's flight. In Scene 5, a Florentine widow and her daughter discuss Bertram's military bravery with their friends.

1 'Set down sharply'

The Countess's instruction at line 33 echoes Helena's 'Write, write' in her letter (line 8). Write the letter that Rinaldo sends to Bertram.

2 Men! (in small groups)

In lines 9–10, Mariana emphasises the importance of chastity. Having seen the pain her mother suffered in childbirth, the goddess Diana (the huntress) decided never to marry, but to preside over the troubles of women. Talk together about what the women in this play have to suffer as a result of men's actions. Widen your debate to consider the situation of women today.

Mariana, Diana and the Widow, Royal Shakespeare Company, 1992.

---

weigh heavy of emphasise
When haply Perhaps when
their ... commander the Sienese
  general

contrary opposite
suffice content
name reputation as a virgin
honesty virginity

94

COUNTESS   What angel shall   25
    Bless this unworthy husband? He cannot thrive,
    Unless her prayers, whom heaven delights to hear
    And loves to grant, reprieve him from the wrath
    Of greatest justice. Write, write, Rinaldo,
    To this unworthy husband of his wife.   30
    Let every word weigh heavy of her worth,
    That he does weigh too light. My greatest grief,
    Though little he do feel it, set down sharply.
    Dispatch the most convenient messenger.
    When haply he shall hear that she is gone,   35
    He will return, and hope I may that she,
    Hearing so much, will speed her foot again,
    Led hither by pure love. Which of them both
    Is dearest to me, I have no skill in sense
    To make distinction. Provide this messenger.   40
    My heart is heavy, and mine age is weak;
    Grief would have tears, and sorrow bids me speak.

Exeunt

ACT 3   SCENE 5
Outside Florence

Trumpet calls far off   Enter old WIDOW *of Florence, her daughter*
DIANA, VIOLENTA, MARIANA *and other Citizens*

WIDOW Nay, come, for if they do approach the city, we shall lose all
    the sight.
DIANA They say the French count has done most honourable service.
WIDOW It is reported that he has taken their great'st commander, and
    that with his own hand he slew the duke's brother.   5
                [*Tucket*]
    We have lost our labour, they are gone a contrary way. Hark! you
    may know by their trumpets.
MARIANA Come, let's return again and suffice ourselves with the report
    of it. Well, Diana, take heed of this French earl. The honour of
    a maid is her name, and no legacy is so rich as honesty.   10

Mariana warns Diana against being seduced. Helena arrives and hears news of Bertram.

1 Beware of men (in pairs)

In Act 2 Scene 1, lines 19–22, the King warned his soldiers against Italian girls. In this scene, it is a girl who is being warned. Compare the two pieces of advice. With whom do you most identify?

2 Mariana's story

Mariana is vehement and detailed in her warning to Diana – perhaps she speaks from personal experience. Imagine you are directing the play. Decide what Mariana's family background is, and what has happened to her in the past. How old is she? She may be a friend of Diana, or of Diana's mother. Who would you cast in the part? Write notes to help the actor to deliver lines 13–22.

3 'Engines of lust'

In lines 15–16, Mariana lists four ways in which men seduce women. Identify them and write a sentence in modern English giving a possible example of each.

solicited propositioned
go under pretend to be
shows in illustrations of
dissuade succession persuade
  other virgins not to be seduced
but that they are limed . . .
  them because they are trapped, as
  birds are by lime on twigs

lie lodge
palmers pilgrims carrying palm
  leaves (to show they have visited
  Jerusalem)
port city gate
ample well

WIDOW I have told my neighbour how you have been solicited by a
    gentleman his companion.
MARIANA I know that knave, hang him! one Parolles, a filthy officer
    he is in those suggestions for the young earl. Beware of them, Diana;
    their promises, enticements, oaths, tokens, and all these engines of   15
    lust, are not the things they go under. Many a maid hath been
    seduced by them, and the misery is, example, that so terrible shows
    in the wrack of maidenhood, cannot for all that dissuade succession,
    but that they are limed with the twigs that threatens them. I hope
    I need not to advise you further, but I hope your own grace will   20
    keep you where you are, though there were no further danger known
    but the modesty which is so lost.
DIANA You shall not need to fear me.

Enter HELENA

WIDOW I hope so. Look, here comes a pilgrim. I know she will lie at
    my house; thither they send one another. I'll question her. God   25
    save you, pilgrim, whither are bound?
HELENA To Saint Jaques le Grand.
    Where do the palmers lodge, I do beseech you?
WIDOW At the Saint Francis here beside the port.
HELENA Is this the way?   30
    A march afar
WIDOW Ay, marry, is't. Hark you, they come this way.
    If you will tarry, holy pilgrim,
    But till the troops come by,
    I will conduct you where you shall be lodged,
    The rather for I think I know your hostess   35
    As ample as myself.
HELENA   Is it yourself?
WIDOW If you shall please so, pilgrim.
HELENA I thank you, and will stay upon your leisure.
WIDOW You came, I think, from France?
HELENA   I did so.
WIDOW Here you shall see a countryman of yours   40
    That has done worthy service.
HELENA   His name, I pray you?
DIANA The Count Rossillion. Know you such a one?
HELENA But by the ear, that hears most nobly of him.
    His face I know not.

The three women discuss Bertram's rejected wife and express sympathy for her. The Widow tells Helena that Bertram is trying to seduce her daughter Diana. The army marches past.

1 'Detesting lord' (in groups of three)

Diana's phrase (line 58) echoes the 'detested wife' of Bertram (Act 2 Scene 3, line 269). Improvise a scene where Parolles tells Diana and the Widow about Bertram and Helena. Make full use of Parolles' typical language. Consider what his motive is for telling them about the situation: mere gossip? to make them pity Bertram? to show that he is a man of the world? to prove himself a good friend to Bertram?

2 You don't mean . . . ?

Decide how Helena speaks lines 61–3. Is she shocked? cunning? pretending to joke? disillusioned? or . . . ?

3 The parade (a whole class activity)

With one person acting as director, work out then stage the army parade. Decide which type of stage you will use: a thrust stage, a proscenium arch, or in the round. Also investigate the way in which the scene could have worked on an Elizabethan stage.

Imagine staging a summer production of the play in your school or college grounds. Decide which area would be most suitable for the parade. Agree on the minimum number of actors you would need to stage an effective march past, and work out how you would do it. In the professional theatre, the high cost of actors' salaries might mean having a smaller parade than you would wish for. What musical instruments would you budget for?

bravely taken highly thought of	**write** call
mere absolutely	**shrewd** hurtful
reservèd honesty strictly preserved chastity	**brokes** bargains like a pimp
examined disputed	**suit** search for love
	Colours military flags

DIANA   Whatsome'er he is,
        He's bravely taken here. He stole from France,   45
        As 'tis reported, for the king had married him
        Against his liking. Think you it is so?
HELENA Ay, surely, mere the truth, I know his lady.
DIANA There is a gentleman that serves the count
        Reports but coarsely of her.
HELENA   What's his name?   50
DIANA Monsieur Parolles.
HELENA   O, I believe with him.
        In argument of praise, or to the worth
        Of the great count himself, she is too mean
        To have her name repeated. All her deserving
        Is a reservèd honesty, and that   55
        I have not heard examined.
DIANA   Alas, poor lady,
        'Tis a hard bondage to become the wife
        Of a detesting lord.
WIDOW I write 'good creature', wheresoe'er she is,
        Her heart weighs sadly. This young maid might do her   60
        A shrewd turn, if she pleased.
HELENA   How do you mean?
        May be the amorous count solicits her
        In the unlawful purpose?
WIDOW   He does indeed,
        And brokes with all that can in such a suit
        Corrupt the tender honour of a maid.   65
        But she is armed for him, and keeps her guard
        In honestest defence.

        Drum and Colours. Enter [BERTRAM] *Count Rossillion,* PAROLLES,
                and the whole army

MARIANA   The gods forbid else!
WIDOW So, now they come.
        That is Antonio, the duke's eldest son,
        That, Escalus.
HELENA   Which is the Frenchman?
DIANA   He,   70
        That with the plume; 'tis a most gallant fellow.
        I would he loved his wife. If he were honester
        He were much goodlier. Is't not a handsome gentleman?

Parolles is miserable about the loss of the drum. Helena will lodge with the Widow, and will advise Diana. In Scene 6, the Second Lord asks Bertram to allow the First Lord to test Parolles' bravery.

1 'That jack-an-apes'

a Parolles is described in the script as a 'hilding' (coward) and a 'bubble'. As you work further through the play, add to this list of insults used to describe him.

b Parolles is described very critically by the Dumaine brothers, yet Bertram has adopted him as a close friend and adviser. Why do you think this is? How old is Parolles? the same age as Bertram? older? much older? When you have come to your own conclusion, read activity 2 on page 110 for a suggestion you may not have thought of.

'The troop is past.'

jack-an-apes showy person
shrewdly bitterly
courtesy curtsey or bow
ring-carrier a go-between, carrying gifts from master to intended female victim
host stay

enjoined penitents people who have promised to go on a pilgrimage to atone for their sins
requite repay
bestow . . . the note give this maiden some worthwhile advice
to't to the test

HELENA I like him well.

DIANA 'Tis pity he is not honest. Yond's that same knave   75
    That leads him to these places. Were I his lady,
    I would poison that vile rascal.

HELENA   Which is he?

DIANA That jack-an-apes with scarfs. Why is he melancholy?

HELENA Perchance he's hurt i'th'battle.

PAROLLES Lose our drum! Well.   80

MARIANA He's shrewdly vexed at something. Look, he has spied us.

WIDOW Marry, hang you!

MARIANA And your courtesy, for a ring-carrier!

                  Exeunt [Bertram, Parolles, and army]

WIDOW The troop is past. Come, pilgrim, I will bring you
    Where you shall host. Of enjoined penitents   85
    There's four or five, to great Saint Jaques bound,
    Already at my house.

HELENA   I humbly thank you.
    Please it this matron and this gentle maid
    To eat with us tonight, the charge and thanking
    Shall be for me, and to requite you further,   90
    I will bestow some precepts of this virgin
    Worthy the note.

BOTH   We'll take your offer kindly.

                           Exeunt

ACT 3   SCENE 6
The Florentine army camp

Enter BERTRAM with the FIRST and SECOND LORDS Dumaine

SECOND LORD Nay, good my lord, put him to't; let him have his way.

FIRST LORD If your lordship find him not a hilding, hold me no more
    in your respect.

SECOND LORD On my life, my lord, a bubble.

BERTRAM Do you think I am so far deceived in him?   5

The Lords Dumaine suggest that Parolles should be persuaded to recover the regiment's captured drum. Soldiers of the Florentine camp will capture him and trick him into revealing his true nature.

1 Let the punishment fit the crime (in pairs)

The drum and flag were very important symbols of a regiment. The loss of the drum in battle is therefore a great dishonour. If you reread the first three lines of Scene 6, it is clear that the Lords Dumaine have all the details of their plot worked out, ready to tell Bertram. Write a short script for, or improvise, the scene where the Lords consider ideas for making Parolles betray himself. The plot must be perfectly tailored to fit Parolles.

2 'A drum so lost!' (in groups of four)

Who does Parolles blame (lines 36–8) for the loss of the drum? Work out from the lines how it was lost. Then take a part each and read aloud lines 31–41. Make each character's attitude clear to the others.

were fit would be advisable
main danger time of great danger
fetch off retrieve
hoodwink blindfold
leaguer camp
examination interrogation
intelligence in his power military
  information he has
the bottom full extent
if . . . John Drum's
  entertainment if you don't throw
  him out (a proverb)
inclining liking for him
sticks . . . disposition annoys you
  greatly
wings flanks

SECOND LORD Believe it, my lord, in mine own direct knowledge, without any malice, but to speak of him as my kinsman, he's a most notable coward, an infinite and endless liar, an hourly promise-breaker, the owner of no one good quality worthy your lordship's entertainment.   10

FIRST LORD It were fit you knew him, lest reposing too far in his virtue, which he hath not, he might at some great and trusty business in a main danger fail you.

BERTRAM I would I knew in what particular action to try him.

FIRST LORD None better than to let him fetch off his drum, which you   15
hear him so confidently undertake to do.

SECOND LORD I, with a troop of Florentines, will suddenly surprise him; such I will have, whom I am sure he knows not from the enemy. We will bind and hoodwink him so, that he shall suppose no other but that he is carried into the leaguer of the adversaries, when we   20
bring him to our own tents. Be but your lordship present at his examination, if he do not, for the promise of his life, and in the highest compulsion of base fear, offer to betray you, and deliver all the intelligence in his power against you, and that with the divine forfeit of his soul upon oath, never trust my judgement in anything.   25

FIRST LORD O, for the love of laughter, let him fetch his drum; he says he has a stratagem for't. When your lordship sees the bottom of his success in't, and to what metal this counterfeit lump of ore will be melted, if you give him not John Drum's entertainment, your inclining cannot be removed. Here he comes.   30

Enter PAROLLES

SECOND LORD O, for the love of laughter, hinder not the honour of his design. Let him fetch off his drum in any hand.

BERTRAM How now, monsieur? This drum sticks sorely in your disposition.

FIRST LORD A pox on't, let it go, 'tis but a drum.   35

PAROLLES But a drum! Is't but a drum? A drum so lost! There was excellent command, to charge in with our horse upon our own wings, and to rend our own soldiers!

FIRST LORD That was not to be blamed in the command of the service; it was a disaster of war that Caesar himself could not have   40
prevented, if he had been there to command.

Parolles is persuaded to recover the regiment's drum that evening. The Lords Dumaine look forward to his undoing.

'By the hand of a soldier.'
Three different Parolles.

hic jacet here lies (a typical inscription on a tomb)
a stomach the courage
mystery skill
magnanimous valiant
pen down my dilemmas write down the possible courses of action

mortal preparation preparation for my death (or preparation of my deadly weapons)
possibility capability
subscribe vouch
invention a tale full of lies
embossed him cornered him

BERTRAM Well, we cannot greatly condemn our success. Some dishonour
we had in the loss of that drum, but it is not to be recovered.

PAROLLES It might have been recovered.

BERTRAM It might, but it is not now.   45

PAROLLES It is to be recovered. But that the merit of service is seldom
attributed to the true and exact performer, I would have that drum
or another, or *hic jacet.*

BERTRAM Why, if you have a stomach, to't, monsieur: if you think your
mystery in stratagem can bring this instrument of honour again   50
into his native quarter, be magnanimous in the enterprise and go
on; I will grace the attempt for a worthy exploit. If you speed well
in it, the duke shall both speak of it, and extend to you what further
becomes his greatness, even to the utmost syllable of your
worthiness.   55

PAROLLES By the hand of a soldier, I will undertake it.

BERTRAM But you must not now slumber in it.

PAROLLES I'll about it this evening, and I will presently pen down my
dilemmas, encourage myself in my certainty, put myself into my
mortal preparation; and by midnight look to hear further from me.   60

BERTRAM May I be bold to acquaint his grace you are gone about it?

PAROLLES I know not what the success will be, my lord, but the attempt
I vow.

BERTRAM I know th'art valiant, and to the possibility of thy soldiership
will subscribe for thee. Farewell.   65

PAROLLES I love not many words.   *Exit*

SECOND LORD No more than a fish loves water. Is not this a strange
fellow, my lord, that so confidently seems to undertake this
business, which he knows is not to be done, damns himself to do,
and dares better be damned than to do't?   70

FIRST LORD You do not know him, my lord, as we do. Certain it is that
he will steal himself into a man's favour, and for a week escape a
great deal of discoveries, but when you find him out, you have him
ever after.

BERTRAM Why, do you think he will make no deed at all of this that   75
so seriously he does address himself unto?

SECOND LORD None in the world, but return with an invention, and
clap upon you two or three probable lies. But we have almost
embossed him, you shall see his fall tonight; for indeed he is not
for your lordship's respect.   80

Bertram will take the First Lord Dumaine to see Diana. She is resisting Bertram's advances. In Scene 7, Helena convinces the Widow that Bertram is her husband.

1 'I sent to her, / By this same coxcomb' (in pairs)

Improvise the scene where Parolles tries unsuccessfully to deliver some 'tokens and letters' from Bertram to Diana. Bring out both Diana's attitude and Parolles' love of the sound of his own voice and high-sounding words.

2 What has Helena said?

a Scene 7 starts in the middle of a conversation. Helena has just told the Widow about her relationship with Bertram. Write a short section of script for the beginning of their 'sworn counsel' (private conversation, with a promise to keep it secret). Include in your script some stage directions to help your actors with both movement and reactions. For example, will tears be appropriate for Helena?

b The Widow seems to accept that Helena is who she says she is (line 14). What has Helena shown her? desperately needed money? or some other token? Decide what seems most likely from what you know of the characters of Helena and the Widow.

3 Men and women

Using only the evidence in the script opposite, what conclusions can you draw from the different ways in which Shakespeare portrays men and women in the play?

---

case unmask
smoked discovered
look my twigs inspect my trap
coxcomb conceited fool
i'th' wind got the scent of

misdoubt me doubt me
But ... work upon except by revealing my identity to Bertram
staining act dishonourable activity

FIRST LORD We'll make you some sport with the fox ere we case him.
He was first smoked by the old Lord Lafew. When his disguise and
he is parted, tell me what a sprat you shall find him, which you
shall see this very night.

SECOND LORD I must go look my twigs. He shall be caught.   85

BERTRAM Your brother, he shall go along with me.

SECOND LORD As't please your lordship. I'll leave you.   [*Exit*]

BERTRAM Now will I lead you to the house, and show you
    The lass I spoke of.

FIRST LORD   But you say she's honest.

BERTRAM That's all the fault. I spoke with her but once,   90
    And found her wondrous cold, but I sent to her,
    By this same coxcomb that we have i'th'wind,
    Tokens and letters which she did re-send,
    And this is all I have done. She's a fair creature;
    Will you go see her?

FIRST LORD   With all my heart, my lord.   95

                             Exeunt

ACT 3   SCENE 7
Florence   The Widow's lodging

Enter HELENA and the WIDOW

HELENA If you misdoubt me that I am not she,
    I know not how I shall assure you further
    But I shall lose the grounds I work upon.

WIDOW Though my estate be fall'n, I was well born,
    Nothing acquainted with these businesses,   5
    And would not put my reputation now
    In any staining act.

HELENA   Nor would I wish you.
    First give me trust, the count he is my husband,
    And what to your sworn counsel I have spoken
    Is so from word to word; and then you cannot,   10
    By the good aid that I of you shall borrow,
    Err in bestowing it.

WIDOW   I should believe you,
    For you have showed me that which well approves
    Y'are great in fortune.

Helena explains her plot. Diana will agree to sleep with Bertram, on the condition that he gives her his family heirloom ring. But on the night, Helena will take Diana's place. The Widow agrees to the plan.

1 Shocks in store for Bertram (a whole class activity)

The Dumaine brothers and Helena are organising plots which will affect Bertram very intimately.

a In lines 18–19, Helena uses war imagery similar to that used by Parolles on page 9. She is planning her campaign to achieve her impossible task. Who do you think will prove the victor in love? Why?

b Members of the audience enjoy knowing something which the characters on-stage do not know. This is called **dramatic irony**. Shakespeare holds the audience's interest and heightens the tension by placing Act 3 Scene 7 before the plot against Parolles begins to unfold. Imagine that you are producing the play, and decide whether or not you want to have an interval here, in order to increase this tension.

c Talk together about the differences between the two plots:
- the difficulty of the tasks
- the cleverness of the plots
- the attitude of those involved – serious or joking.

2 A seduction has been arranged . . .
(in pairs or groups of three)

How do you think Diana will react when her mother informs her of what she has agreed with Helena? She may resent being told what to do, or she may be pleased with the money (some now, the rest afterwards, as a marriage dowry). Perhaps she will add suggestions of her own. Improvise the imagined scene.

found received	**idle fire** mad lust
wanton lecherous	**To marry her** as a dowry
carry conquer	**persèver** behave
in fine in the end	**prove coherent** fit in
important blood lust	**nothing steads us** does us no good
county Bertram	**assay** try
rich choice high regard	**speed** succeed

HELENA   Take this purse of gold,
          And let me buy your friendly help thus far,   15
          Which I will over-pay and pay again
          When I have found it. The count he woos your daughter,
          Lays down his wanton siege before her beauty,
          Resolved to carry her. Let her in fine consent,
          As we'll direct her how 'tis best to bear it.   20
          Now his important blood will naught deny
          That she'll demand. A ring the county wears,
          That downward hath succeeded in his house
          From son to son, some four or five descents,
          Since the first father wore it. This ring he holds   25
          In most rich choice; yet in his idle fire,
          To buy his will, it would not seem too dear,
          Howe'er repented after.
WIDOW   Now I see
          The bottom of your purpose.
HELENA You see it lawful then. It is no more   30
          But that your daughter, ere she seems as won,
          Desires this ring; appoints him an encounter;
          In fine, delivers me to fill the time,
          Herself most chastely absent. After,
          To marry her, I'll add three thousand crowns   35
          To what is passed already.
WIDOW   I have yielded.
          Instruct my daughter how she shall persèver,
          That time and place with this deceit so lawful
          May prove coherent. Every night he comes
          With musics of all sorts, and songs composed   40
          To her unworthiness. It nothing steads us
          To chide him from our eaves, for he persists
          As if his life lay on't.
HELENA   Why then tonight
          Let us assay our plot, which if it speed,
          Is wicked meaning in a lawful deed,   45
          And lawful meaning in a lawful act,
          Where both not sin, and yet a sinful fact.
          But let's about it.
                                                      [*Exeunt*]

Looking back at Act 3
Activities for groups and individuals

1 To cut, or not to cut?

Some directors cut Act 3 Scene 1. Take sides and argue for and against cutting this 'Duke of Florence' scene from your production. List your reasons for and against under headings such as: information given, dramatic effect, character, and the structure of the play.

2 Parolles and Bertram – two views

The Polish director, Konrad Swinarski, said about his production of *All's Well*:

> ... the first thing I discovered is that the whole story between Bertram and Parolles is really a homosexual story, which is based on the intrigue of Lafew to get Parolles for himself, to deliver Bertram from Parolles, and to be useful to the King in this way while suiting his own interests.

Harriet Walter, who played Helena in the 1981 Royal Shakespeare Company production, said:

> The bigger influence in Bertram's life is the older man, Parolles, who's a wastrel, a braggart-buffoon. *Everybody* sees through Parolles. Someone calls him a 'window of lattice'. But not Bertram, because Parolles appeals to his ego and makes him feel like a man. Parolles is a kind of father-substitute – Bertram's father has just died – except that Parolles doesn't fit Bertram's world.

Find evidence in the script which leads you to agree or disagree with these views. Write your own account of how the friendship between the two men begins and develops.

3 The Dumaine brothers – which is which?

In some productions, the Dumaine brothers have appeared as twins. If you were a director, how would you distinguish between the two? Consider mannerisms, costume, voice and other differences. Look at the photographs on pages 16, 50, 80, 130, 136 and 146, in which the

Dumaine brothers appear. Try to pick out the brothers in each group. Each photograph shows a different designer's view of the brothers.

4 A pilgrim's journey?

Is Helena chasing Bertram? If Helena is on a pilgrimage to Spain, what is she doing in Florence? Did she happen to end up there, or has she deliberately followed Bertram? Angela Down, who played Helena in the BBC television production, said:

> When everybody says how honest she is, you've got to believe that, in fact, she is. At the same time, I don't think there's any doubt that she's an opportunist. She knows that she's got the power to cure the King, but it never occurs to her to do so until Bertram goes to court – and she admits as much. As soon as it does occur to her, off she goes and does it, gets Bertram – end of plan. *That* doesn't work out, so she says (quite genuinely, I'm sure): 'Well, I must get away from France because I've done a terrible thing'. In Act 3 Scene 2, she says: 'Oh, what have I done? Isn't it awful? Now he's going off, possibly to get killed, and it's because of me, so the best thing I can do is leave so he can come home'. But the next thing she does is go to Florence, the very place where he is, so you think: 'Well, that's a funny place to go if you want to get out of his hair!'. But you often find in life, don't you, that you're saying and *meaning* one thing, but you find you're *doing* something that is facilitating an event which might turn the tables. She puts herself in the way of opportunities, and then when they arrive, she takes full advantage of them. Nothing wrong with that! But she isn't by any means just a total innocent abroad!

Talk together about what you think of Angela Down's viewpoint. Do you think Helena is calculating? The play has many elements of fairy-tale in it – perhaps Shakespeare had not really considered geography very seriously and saw Helena's journey as part of the fantasy.

5 A problem for the stage manager

Act 3 contains seven scenes. Consider how you could indicate the various places without slowing down the action with extensive scene changes.

Parolles' ambush is prepared. His captors plan to speak in an invented foreign language. Parolles wonders when he can reasonably return to camp – and what his story should be.

1 Springing the trap (in small groups)

a Although the Second Lord Dumaine is plotting closely with the soldiers, he is above them in social status. How can this difference be shown in manners and behaviour?

b As director, draw a diagram to plan how the ambush is to be staged. A situation has to be set up in which the soldiers can observe Parolles without his knowledge, so careful positioning of all the actors will be necessary. The soldiers could be hidden by bushes, or move behind their victim as he moves. Talk together about the problems posed by using different types of acting space, for example, an in-the-round or a thrust stage.

c There are similar 'gulling' situations in *Much Ado About Nothing* Act 2 Scene 3, and Act 3 Scene 1, and *Twelfth Night* Act 2 Scene 5. In each case someone is tricked while being watched by those organising the plot. When you have worked through the scene of the 'gulling' of Parolles, find copies of the two other Shakespeare plays and compare the 'gulling' scenes in each.

d Write notes to advise Parolles on how he should enter and speak his first six lines.

---

sally upon rush out on
linsey-woolsey mixed-up language (literally: linen-wool cloth)
adversary's entertainment service of the enemy
smack smattering

choughs' language jackdaws' chattering
politic cunning
couch ho lie low
plausive invention believable lie
smoke suspect

ACT 4 SCENE 1
Near the Florentine army camp

Enter the SECOND LORD *Dumaine with five or six other soldiers ready to ambush*

SECOND LORD He can come no other way but by this hedge corner. When you sally upon him, speak what terrible language you will. Though you understand it not yourselves, no matter; for we must not seem to understand him, unless some one among us, whom we must produce for an interpreter. 5

FIRST SOLDIER Good captain, let me be th'interpreter.

SECOND LORD Art not acquainted with him? Knows he not thy voice?

FIRST SOLDIER No, sir, I warrant you.

SECOND LORD But what linsey-woolsey hast thou to speak to us again?

FIRST SOLDIER E'en such as you speak to me. 10

SECOND LORD He must think us some band of strangers i'th'adversary's entertainment. Now he hath a smack of all neighbouring languages; therefore we must every one be a man of his own fancy, not to know what we speak to one another; so we seem to know, is to know straight our purpose: choughs' language, gabble enough, and good 15 enough. As for you, interpreter, you must seem very politic. But couch ho, here he comes, to beguile two hours in a sleep, and then to return and swear the lies he forges.

Enter PAROLLES

PAROLLES Ten a'clock: within these three hours 'twill be time enough to go home. What shall I say I have done? It must be a very plausive 20 invention that carries it. They begin to smoke me, and disgraces have of late knocked too often at my door. I find my tongue is too foolhardy, but my heart hath the fear of Mars before it, and of his creatures, not daring the reports of my tongue.

SECOND LORD This is the first truth that e'er thine own tongue was 25 guilty of.

Parolles sees that his boasting has led him into danger. He resolves to keep quiet in future, and wonders how he can make himself seem injured without hurting himself. The soldiers ambush and blindfold him.

1 The cowardly hero (in pairs)

Act out Parolles' debate with himself (lines 27–49) in the following ways:

a One of you takes the part of Parolles, while the other directs the action. Just use Parolles' lines, leaving out the Second Lord Dumaine. Give as much visual impact as you can to the language. For example, you could act out each of his suggestions.

b Take a role each. This time include Lord Dumaine's words, but assume that Parolles cannot hear anything the Lord says.

c Speak all the lines again. This time, Parolles overhears some of the Second Lord's comments. Will Parolles be surprised to hear a voice in the air, or will he think it is simply a continuation of his own thoughts? Work out how you will achieve maximum humour on lines 45–6, where Parolles answers the Lord's question.

d After your experiments with **a**, **b** and **c**, decide which is the most dramatically effective way of staging this episode.

2 Any suggestions?

Lines 32–3 (Tongue . . . mule) seem to mean: 'I will give my tongue away to a garrulous dairymaid and buy a silent one which will not get me into trouble'. No one really knows what Bajazeth's mule refers to – it may be a misprint for 'mute', as Bajazeth was a Turkish prince strangled, on his father's orders, by royal mutes (silent servants). Any ideas?

---

baring of shaving off
in stratagem a cunning plan
Muskos' (perhaps) Muscovites'

discover reveal
undo ruin

PAROLLES What the devil should move me to undertake the recovery
of this drum, being not ignorant of the impossibility, and knowing
I had no such purpose? I must give myself some hurts, and say
I got them in exploit. Yet slight ones will not carry it. They will   30
say, 'Came you off with so little?' And great ones I dare not give;
wherefore what's the instance? Tongue, I must put you into a
butter-woman's mouth, and buy myself another of Bajazeth's mule,
if you prattle me into these perils.

SECOND LORD Is it possible he should know what he is, and be that   35
he is?

PAROLLES I would the cutting of my garments would serve the turn,
or the breaking of my Spanish sword.

SECOND LORD We cannot afford you so.

PAROLLES Or the baring of my beard, and to say it was in stratagem.   40

SECOND LORD 'Twould not do.

PAROLLES Or to drown my clothes, and say I was stripped.

SECOND LORD Hardly serve.

PAROLLES Though I swore I leapt from the window of the citadel –

SECOND LORD How deep?   45

PAROLLES Thirty fathom.

SECOND LORD Three great oaths would scarce make that be believed.

PAROLLES I would I had any drum of the enemy's. I would swear I
recovered it.

SECOND LORD You shall hear one anon.   50

PAROLLES A drum now of the enemy's –

Alarum within

SECOND LORD *Throca movousus, cargo, cargo, cargo.*

ALL *Cargo, cargo, cargo, villianda par corbo, cargo.*

PAROLLES O ransom, ransom! Do not hide mine eyes.

[*They blindfold him*]

INTERPRETER *Boskos thromuldo boskos.*   55

PAROLLES I know you are the Muskos' regiment,
And I shall lose my life for want of language.
If there be here German, or Dane, Low Dutch,
Italian, or French, let him speak to me,
I'll discover that which shall undo the Florentine.   60

Parolles' captors tell him that his life is in danger. To save his life, Parolles offers to betray the Florentines. The Second Lord Dumaine sends for Bertram to come and hear Parolles' betrayal.

1 Nonsense language (in groups of three)

The Second Lord Dumaine has told each of his soldiers to invent his own language to deceive Parolles. (It is ironic that Parolles, whose name means 'words', should be tricked by meaningless words.)

a Make up your own 'nonsense' language and have a conversation. You will be surprised how much sense you can make to one another, with the help of your tone of voice and facial expressions. Now try your invented conversation again, this time as Parolles experiences it – blindfolded.

b Invent a few 'Muskos-English' dictionary entries, to enable someone to 'translate' Shakespeare's invented language. Let your imagination run!

2 'Seventeen poniards' (a whole class activity)

Create a 'frozen picture' to illustrate the seventeen daggers pointed at Parolles' chest. Aim to make the scene as funny as possible. One student suggested that the soldiers would be relaxing around the stage, nowhere near Parolles. Another idea was to touch him with just one twig. Parolles is so frightened that his imagination will make him believe almost anything.

---

betake thee to thy faith say your prayers
poniards daggers
hoodwinked blindfolded and deceived

Haply perhaps
space a reprieve
woodcock stupid bird

INTERPRETER *Boskos vauvado.* I understand thee, and can speak thy
    tongue. *Kerelybonto*, sir, betake thee to thy faith, for seventeen
    poniards are at thy bosom.
PAROLLES O!
INTERPRETER O, pray, pray, pray! *Manka revania dulche.* 65
SECOND LORD *Oscorbidulchos volivorco.*
INTERPRETER The general is content to spare thee yet,
    And hoodwinked as thou art, will lead thee on
    To gather from thee. Haply thou mayst inform
    Something to save thy life.
PAROLLES   O, let me live, 70
    And all the secrets of our camp I'll show,
    Their force, their purposes; nay, I'll speak that
    Which you will wonder at.
INTERPRETER   But wilt thou faithfully?
PAROLLES If I do not, damn me.
INTERPRETER   *Acordo linta.*
    Come on, thou art granted space. 75
                                    Exit [with Parolles]
                A short alarum within
SECOND LORD Go tell the Count Rossillion, and my brother,
    We have caught the woodcock, and will keep him muffled
    Till we do hear from them.
SOLDIER   Captain, I will.
SECOND LORD 'A will betray us all unto ourselves:
    Inform on that.
SOLDIER   So I will, sir. 80
SECOND LORD Till then I'll keep him dark and safely locked.
                                    Exeunt

Bertram begins to woo Diana with flattery. She reminds him of his duty to Helena. He insists that he will love Diana for ever, but she doubts whether love will outlast lust.

1 Wooing (in pairs)

The page opposite is written in verse. Several of the lines are 'split lines' (shared between the two characters). Taking a part each, read the scene aloud. Many actors and directors believe that to keep the rhythm of the verse you must not pause in a split line, and this moves the scene along very quickly. Experiment with different ways of speaking lines 1–20. Try making pauses of varying lengths in the split lines. Discover what effect your various methods of speaking the lines have on the mood of the scene.

Diana and Bertram, Stratford, 1989.

Diana's image of the rose is a reminder of the Countess's words in Act 1 Scene 3, lines 101–3. How apt do you think the image (lines 17–19) is in the conversation between Bertram and Diana?

Fontybell beauteous fountain	**honest** virtuous
quality part	**vows** resolution to live away from
quick lively	Helena
got conceived	**serve** satisfy sexually

ACT 4   SCENE 2
Florence   The Widow's lodging

Enter BERTRAM and DIANA

BERTRAM They told me that your name was Fontybell.
DIANA No, my good lord, Diana.
BERTRAM   Titled goddess,
    And worth it, with addition! But, fair soul,
    In your fine frame hath love no quality?
    If the quick fire of youth light not your mind,   5
    You are no maiden, but a monument.
    When you are dead, you should be such a one
    As you are now; for you are cold and stern,
    And now you should be as your mother was
    When your sweet self was got.   10
DIANA She then was honest.
BERTRAM   So should you be.
DIANA   No;
    My mother did but duty, such, my lord,
    As you owe to your wife.
BERTRAM   No more a' that.
    I prithee do not strive against my vows.
    I was compelled to her, but I love thee   15
    By love's own sweet constraint, and will for ever
    Do thee all rights of service.
DIANA   Ay, so you serve us
    Till we serve you; but when you have our roses,
    You barely leave our thorns to prick ourselves,
    And mock us with our bareness.
BERTRAM   How have I sworn!   20

In Diana's opinion, Bertram's vows of love are worthless. He continues his attempt to sleep with her. She asks for his ring. He tells her of its importance in his family, but finally gives it to her.

1 'Be not so holy-cruel'

Suggest some advice you could give to the actor playing Diana. Do you see her as cheeky? demure? teasing? or . . . ?

2 'Men make rope's in such a scarre' – help!

No one is sure what is meant by line 38. Shakespeare's handwriting may have been misread. Some scholars think this is the most obscure line in all Shakespeare. Here are some of their suggested meanings: may rope us in such a snare/make vows in such a flame/make hopes in such affairs/make hopes in such a scene. You may think these are as confusing as the original. Assist Shakespeare scholarship and think of something clearer!

3 Turning the tables (in pairs)

a Taking a part each, read lines 38–53. Talk together about the way Diana uses Bertram's own language (particularly the use of the word 'honour') to overthrow his arguments.

b Diana reads aloud her lines 45–9, and Bertram reacts in an appropriate way. Decide whether he looks guilty, annoyed or frustrated in his desires – or if he has some other expression.

4 'Here, take my ring!' (in pairs)

Experiment with varous ways of staging lines 51–3, making the moment as humorous as possible. Will Bertram throw the ring to Diana? go down on his knees? accidentally drop it in his excitement? or . . . ?

---

the High'st / Him God
I did love you ill I didn't love you
holding conviction
protest profess
words . . . but unsealed empty
  words and a worthless contract
  (without a legal seal)

crafts craftiness
persèver continue
'longing belonging
obloquy disgrace
proper personal
part side

DIANA 'Tis not the many oaths that makes the truth,
But the plain single vow that is vowed true.
What is not holy, that we swear not by,
But take the High'st to witness. Then pray you tell me,
If I should swear by Jove's great attributes   25
I loved you dearly, would you believe my oaths
When I did love you ill? This has no holding,
To swear by Him whom I protest to love
That I will work against Him. Therefore your oaths
Are words and poor conditions, but unsealed –   30
At least in my opinion.
BERTRAM   Change it, change it!
Be not so holy-cruel. Love is holy,
And my integrity ne'er knew the crafts
That you do charge men with. Stand no more off,
But give thyself unto my sick desires,   35
Who then recovers. Say thou art mine, and ever
My love, as it begins, shall so persèver.
DIANA I see that men make rope's in such a scarre,
That we'll forsake ourselves. Give me that ring.
BERTRAM I'll lend it thee, my dear; but have no power   40
To give it from me.
DIANA   Will you not, my lord?
BERTRAM It is an honour 'longing to our house,
Bequeathèd down from many ancestors,
Which were the greatest obloquy i'th'world
In me to lose.
DIANA   Mine honour's such a ring,   45
My chastity's the jewel of our house,
Bequeathèd down from many ancestors,
Which were the greatest obloquy i'th'world
In me to lose. Thus your own proper wisdom
Brings in the champion Honour on my part,   50
Against your vain assault.
BERTRAM   Here, take my ring!
My house, mine honour, yea, my life, be thine,
And I'll be bid by thee.

Diana tells Bertram to come to her bed that night, but not speak. Alone, she reflects on the truth of her mother's predictions. In Scene 3, the Lords note how the Countess's letter disturbs Bertram.

1 The bed trick (in pairs)

Helena has tried to ensure that Bertram will not discover that he is in bed with his own wife. He must not speak to her in bed, and the whole business must last no longer than an hour.

a Talk together about what could go wrong with the plan.

b Do you think that Helena's actions are justified? (Remember, she has involved the Widow and Diana in her deceit.)

2 Exit lines (in small groups)

a Experiment with ways in which Bertram could deliver line 66. For example, lustfully? with a kiss? romantically? triumphantly?

b Diana's line 67 as Bertram leaves, has a double meaning. Line 68, when she is alone, suggests a different tone. Decide how to speak these two lines.

3 A girl's best friend is her mother

What exactly has Diana's mother told her (lines 69–71)? Write a short scene in which the Widow remembers her own experiences with men.

4 'How have I sworn!'

Diana recalls that Bertram has 'sworn to marry me/When his wife's dead'. There are no lines in the script to cover this promise. As a director, how and when would you show it?

I'll order take I will make sure
band promise
that what in time . . . deeds if I become pregnant, the ring will prove you are the father
she sat in's heart she could read his mind

braid twisted (like braid or plaited hair)
Marry that will whoever else wants to marry
cozen deceive
worthy well deserved

DIANA When midnight comes, knock at my chamber window;
  I'll order take my mother shall not hear.   55
  Now will I charge you in the band of truth,
  When you have conquered my yet maiden bed,
  Remain there but an hour, nor speak to me.
  My reasons are most strong, and you shall know them
  When back again this ring shall be delivered; 60
  And on your finger in the night I'll put
  Another ring, that what in time proceeds
  May token to the future our past deeds.
  Adieu till then, then fail not. You have won
  A wife of me, though there my hope be done. 65
BERTRAM A heaven on earth I have won by wooing thee. *Exit*
DIANA For which live long to thank both heaven and me!
  You may so in the end.
  My mother told me just how he would woo,
  As if she sat in's heart. She says all men 70
  Have the like oaths. He had sworn to marry me
  When his wife's dead; therefore I'll lie with him
  When I am buried. Since Frenchmen are so braid,
  Marry that will, I live and die a maid.
  Only in this disguise I think't no sin 75
  To cozen him that would unjustly win. *Exit*

ACT 4   SCENE 3
The Florentine army camp

Enter the FIRST *and* SECOND LORDS *Dumaine with two or three*
soldiers

FIRST LORD You have not given him his mother's letter?
SECOND LORD I have delivered it an hour since. There is something
 in't that stings his nature; for on the reading it he changed almost
 into another man.
FIRST LORD He has much worthy blame laid upon him for shaking off 5
 so good a wife and so sweet a lady.

Bertram has displeased the King and seduced Diana. The Lords will wait for Bertram before dealing with Parolles. They wonder what Bertram will do now that peace has been made. The First Lord reports Helena's death.

---

1 The brothers Dumaine (in small groups)

a Imagine you are directing this scene. Decide where you will set it, and what you will have the brothers doing. They could be playing cards, preparing their weapons, or sorting out maps.

b The Dumaines' conversation in Scene 3 is rich in imagery. For example, 'fleshes his will' and 'dieted to his hour' suggest pictures of eating, as well as of sexual intercourse. 'Anatomised', 'measure' and 'counterfeit' use images of accuracy and honesty in reference to Parolles. Talk together about the aptness of the brothers' language and imagery.

2 'His own nobility'

In lines 17–22, the Lords suggest that, by ignoring God, Bertram is not behaving in an honourable way appropriate to his noble station in life. How far do you agree with their judgement?

3 'So sweet a lady'

Using the script opposite and on page 123, list the words and phrases used by the First Lord Dumaine to describe Helena. How complete do you think this picture of her is?

4 What has been happening? (in pairs)

Much information is given in this conversation. Imagine that you have overheard it. In your own words, report what you have learnt to a fellow soldier.

---

tuned his bounty extended his generosity
monumental ancestral
himself made he has proved his manhood
composition bargain
delay our rebellion make us slow to sin

As we are ourselves without God's help
dieted . . . hour limited to an hour (for his seduction)
anatomised dissected
pretence intention
in fine in short

SECOND LORD Especially he hath incurred the everlasting displeasure
of the king, who had even tuned his bounty to sing happiness to
him. I will tell you a thing, but you shall let it dwell darkly with
you.   10

FIRST LORD When you have spoken it, 'tis dead, and I am the grave
of it.

SECOND LORD He hath perverted a young gentlewoman here in
Florence, of a most chaste renown, and this night he fleshes his will
in the spoil of her honour. He hath given her his monumental ring,   15
and thinks himself made in the unchaste composition.

FIRST LORD Now God delay our rebellion! As we are ourselves, what
things are we!

SECOND LORD Merely our own traitors. And as in the common course
of all treasons, we still see them reveal themselves, till they attain   20
to their abhorred ends, so he that in this action contrives against
his own nobility in his proper stream o'erflows himself.

FIRST LORD Is it not meant damnable in us, to be trumpeters of our
unlawful intents? We shall not then have his company tonight?

SECOND LORD Not till after midnight; for he is dieted to his hour.   25

FIRST LORD That approaches apace. I would gladly have him see his
company anatomised, that he might take a measure of his own
judgements, wherein so curiously he had set this counterfeit.

SECOND LORD We will not meddle with him till he come; for his
presence must be the whip of the other.   30

FIRST LORD In the mean time, what hear you of these wars?

SECOND LORD I hear there is an overture of peace.

FIRST LORD Nay, I assure you a peace concluded.

SECOND LORD What will Count Rossillion do then? Will he travel
higher, or return again into France?   35

FIRST LORD I perceive by this demand, you are not altogether of his
council.

SECOND LORD Let it be forbid, sir. So should I be a great deal of his
act.

FIRST LORD Sir, his wife some two months since fled from his house.   40
Her pretence is a pilgrimage to Saint Jaques le Grand, which holy
undertaking with most austere sanctimony she accomplished; and
there residing, the tenderness of her nature became as a prey to her
grief; in fine, made a groan of her last breath, and now she sings
in heaven.   45

The Lords fear Bertram will be glad that Helena is dead. They discuss the mixture of good and bad in human nature. A servant says Bertram will leave for France the next day. Bertram describes all he has just done.

1 Spear carriers

Small roles in a play are especially difficult to act and to time well. There is not long to make a lasting impression on an audience. If you were playing the servant in this scene, how would you approach it? Many directors double parts to save actors' wages, just as Shakespeare's company did. If you wanted to double here, which other role or roles could the servant play?

2 'Sixteen businesses'

Write out in your own words a summary of what Bertram has been doing (lines 73–7).

3 Watch your language

'Effected many nicer needs' (lines 76–7) is Bertram's delicate way of saying: 'I have seduced a virgin'. Are you surprised by his language at this point, after the way he has expressed himself earlier in the play? Experiment with several ways of delivering this line, for example: with an accompanying wink, leeringly, triumphantly, delicately.

4 Just a line to say . . .

Bertram has sent a letter to his mother to tell her of Helena's death. Remembering the tone of his earlier letters, what do you think he will have written?

---

justified verified
intelligence information
to the full arming of the verity undeniable proof
They shall . . . commend the letters will be most necessary, even if they exaggerate Bertram's good points (as he has upset the King)

by an abstract of success to give a summary of my success
congied with taken my leave of
entertained my convoy made my travel arrangements
parcels of dispatch matters to be settled

SECOND LORD How is this justified?

FIRST LORD The stronger part of it by her own letters, which makes
her story true, even to the point of her death. Her death itself, which
could not be her office to say is come, was faithfully confirmed by
the rector of the place.   50

SECOND LORD Hath the count all this intelligence?

FIRST LORD Ay, and the particular confirmations, point from point, to
the full arming of the verity.

SECOND LORD I am heartily sorry that he'll be glad of this.

FIRST LORD How mightily sometimes we make us comforts of our   55
losses!

SECOND LORD And how mightily some other times we drown our gain
in tears! The great dignity that his valour hath here acquired for
him shall at home be encountered with a shame as ample.

FIRST LORD The web of our life is of a mingled yarn, good and ill   60
together: our virtues would be proud, if our faults whipped them
not, and our crimes would despair, if they were not cherished by
our virtues.

Enter a [SERVANT as] Messenger

How now? where's your master?

SERVANT He met the duke in the street, sir, of whom he hath taken   65
a solemn leave. His lordship will next morning for France. The duke
hath offered him letters of commendations to the king.

SECOND LORD They shall be no more than needful there, if they were
more than they can commend.

Enter [BERTRAM] Count Rossillion

FIRST LORD They cannot be too sweet for the king's tartness. Here's   70
his lordship now. How now, my lord, is't not after midnight?

BERTRAM I have tonight dispatched sixteen businesses, a month's
length apiece, by an abstract of success: I have congied with the
duke, done my adieu with his nearest; buried a wife, mourned for
her, writ to my lady mother I am returning, entertained my convoy,   75
and between these main parcels of dispatch effected many nicer
needs. The last was the greatest, but that I have not ended yet.

SECOND LORD If the business be of any difficulty, and this morning
your departure hence, it requires haste of your lordship.

Bertram fears he may hear more of Diana. After a night in the stocks, Parolles is brought in. His interrogation begins. He reveals the numbers of the Duke's cavalry and says they are poor soldiers.

1 Bertram's fear

Bertram's lines 80–1 suggest that he thinks Diana may later claim him as her husband. How surprised are you to find him trying, so soon, to wriggle out of his promise to marry her if Helena dies?

2 'Do not hide mine eyes' (a whole class activity)

Parolles is blindfolded and will feel disorientated. He has been weeping. Do you have any sympathy for him? Try the following activity and see if it makes you sympathetic.

Divide into pairs, **A** and **B**. **A**, close your eyes and allow **B** to lead you by the hand round the room. **B**, be very careful to ensure that **A** trusts you. When **A** feels secure, try leading by just the touch of a fingertip. Reverse roles. How did you feel? Are you now more sympathetic towards Parolles?

If you have space and a brave volunteer, try a second activity. The volunteer is blindfolded and put in the centre of the space. Other members of the group try at random to disorientate the 'victim' by, for example, whispering to, or gently turning them. The 'victim' then shares their experience of the situation with the group. The object is not to frighten the wits out of the victim (being blindfolded is upsetting enough), but to show how little you have to do to unsettle someone.

3 'I'll take the sacrament on't'

Parolles denigrates the Florentine troops (lines 110–12). Do you think this is his real (perhaps cynical) opinion, or is he saying what he thinks his captors want to hear?

---

counterfeit module imitation soldier
usurping his spurs wearing a soldier's emblem he had no right to
Muffled blindfolded
Hoodman blindfolded for blindman's-buff

constraint compulsion
out of a note from a list of questions
I'll take . . . you will I'll swear on the Holy Sacrament, according to any religious rites you follow
past-saving out and out

BERTRAM I mean the business is not ended, as fearing to hear of it   80
    hereafter. But shall we have this dialogue between the fool and the
    soldier? Come, bring forth this counterfeit module, h'as deceived
    me like a double-meaning prophesier.
SECOND LORD Bring him forth.

                                       [Exeunt Soldiers]

    H'as sat in th'stocks all night, poor gallant knave.   85
BERTRAM No matter, his heels have deserved it, in usurping his spurs
    so long. How does he carry himself?
SECOND LORD I have told your lordship already: the stocks carry him.
    But to answer you as you would be understood, he weeps like a
    wench that had shed her milk. He hath confessed himself to   90
    Morgan, whom he supposes to be a friar, from the time of his
    remembrance to this very instant disaster of his setting i'th'stocks;
    and what think you he hath confessed?
BERTRAM Nothing of me, has'a?
SECOND LORD His confession is taken, and it shall be read to his face.   95
    If your lordship be in't, as I believe you are, you must have the
    patience to hear it.

          Enter PAROLLES *with his* INTERPRETER

BERTRAM A plague upon him! Muffled! He can say nothing of me.
FIRST LORD Hush, hush! Hoodman comes! *Portotartarossa.*
INTERPRETER He calls for the tortures. What will you say without 'em?   100
PAROLLES I will confess what I know without constraint. If ye pinch
    me like a pasty, I can say no more.
INTERPRETER *Bosko chimurcho.*
FIRST LORD *Boblibindo chicurmurco.*
INTERPRETER You are a merciful general. Our general bids you answer   105
    to what I shall ask you out of a note.
PAROLLES And truly, as I hope to live.
INTERPRETER [*Reads*] 'First demand of him, how many horse the duke
    is strong.' What say you to that?
PAROLLES Five or six thousand, but very weak and unserviceable. The   110
    troops are all scattered, and the commanders very poor rogues, upon
    my reputation and credit, and as I hope to live.
INTERPRETER Shall I set down your answer so?
PAROLLES Do, I'll take the sacrament on't, how and which way you
    will.   115
BERTRAM All's one to him. What a past-saving slave is this!

Parolles continues to give away military secrets. He says the cavalry are weak and the infantry useless. He claims that the First Lord Dumaine is a low-class lecher.

Blindfolded Parolles.

1 Parolles betrays his fellow soldiers (in small groups)

The photograph above comes from a production staged in 1959, but set in the Second World War. Many of the audience would have been affected by that fairly recent war. Talk together about how you think they would have felt about the production. Do you think they would have felt appalled by Parolles' betrayal of his comrades, or would they have felt sympathetic towards him?

chape metal cover
set down recorded
But I con . . . delivers it I don't
 thank him for speaking the truth
afoot in the infantry
muster-file total number on roll
pole soldiers (a poll is a head count)

cassocks military cloaks
the particular . . . inter'gatories
 each item of the list separately
botcher's prentice apprentice to a
 repairman
shrieve's fool feeble-minded girl
 in the Sheriff's care

FIRST LORD Y'are deceived, my lord, this is Monsieur Parolles, the
gallant militarist – that was his own phrase – that had the whole
theoric of war in the knot of his scarf, and the practice in the chape
of his dagger.   120

SECOND LORD I will never trust a man again for keeping his sword
clean, nor believe he can have everything in him by wearing his
apparel neatly.

INTERPRETER Well, that's set down.

PAROLLES 'Five or six thousand horse', I said – I will say true – 'or   125
thereabouts', set down, for I'll speak truth.

FIRST LORD He's very near the truth in this.

BERTRAM But I con him no thanks for't, in the nature he delivers it.

PAROLLES 'Poor rogues', I pray you say.

INTERPRETER Well, that's set down.   130

PAROLLES I humbly thank you, sir. A truth's a truth, the rogues are
marvellous poor.

INTERPRETER [Reads] 'Demand of him, of what strength they are
afoot.' What say you to that?

PAROLLES By my troth, sir, if I were to live this present hour, I will   135
tell true. Let me see: Spurio, a hundred and fifty; Sebastian, so
many; Corambus, so many; Jaques, so many; Guiltian, Cosmo,
Lodowick, and Gratii, two hundred fifty each; mine own company,
Chitopher, Vaumond, Bentii, two hundred fifty each; so that the
muster-file, rotten and sound, upon my life, amounts not to fifteen   140
thousand pole, half of the which dare not shake the snow from off
their cassocks, lest they shake themselves to pieces.

BERTRAM What shall be done to him?

FIRST LORD Nothing, but let him have thanks. Demand of him my
condition, and what credit I have with the duke.   145

INTERPRETER Well, that's set down. [Reads] 'You shall demand of
him, whether one Captain Dumaine be i'th'camp, a Frenchman;
what his reputation is with the duke; what his valour, honesty, and
expertness in wars; or whether he thinks it were not possible with
well-weighing sums of gold to corrupt him to a revolt.' What say   150
you to this? What do you know of it?

PAROLLES I beseech you let me answer to the particular of the
inter'gatories. Demand them singly.

INTERPRETER Do you know this Captain Dumaine?

PAROLLES I know him. 'A was a botcher's prentice in Paris, from   155
whence he was whipped for getting the shrieve's fool with child,
a dumb innocent that could not say him nay.

Parolles says the Duke wrote to tell him to dismiss the First Lord from the army. A letter from Parolles to Diana is found and read. It warns Diana to take her payment before she promises Bertram anything.

1 A true friend . . .

Parolles has been Bertram's chief friend and adviser in his personal and professional life. If you were playing the role of Bertram, how would you react as the letter to Diana is read? (Remember, you are surrounded by fellow soldiers and will want to 'save face' as far as possible.)

2 'Not the duke's letter'

Parolles' letter is written in rhymed verse and contains *double entendres*, sometimes of a sexual nature (such as 'score'). You will remember from his conversation with Helena in Act 1 that he is fond of talking about sex. What do you think was his motive in writing the letter to Diana? Why wasn't it sent?

3 'Thine, as he vowed to thee' (in pairs)

Think about how Parolles may have behaved when he first met Diana, probably in Bertram's company.

Either: improvise a scene where Parolles takes Bertram's message, but tries to woo Diana for himself.

Or: improvise a scene where Diana tells Mariana or her mother about Parolles' behaviour.

4 A peculiar punishment?

In lines 196–7, Bertram suggests whipping Parolles through the camp with the damning description of Bertram's behaviour written on his forehead. On reflection, Bertram may not want such a description circulated so widely. Devise a more appropriate punishment.

---

his brains . . . falls this liar is likely to die at any moment
an advertisement some advice
ruttish lustful
whale . . . finds has an insatiable appetite for virgins

fry small young fish (girls)
Half won is match well made make your bargain first and you are halfway to success
mell meddle (have sex)
For count of so take note of

BERTRAM Nay, by your leave, hold your hands – though I know his
    brains are forfeit to the next tile that falls.

INTERPRETER Well, is this captain in the Duke of Florence's camp?   160

PAROLLES Upon my knowledge, he is, and lousy.

FIRST LORD Nay, look not so upon me; we shall hear of your lordship
    anon.

INTERPRETER What is his reputation with the duke?

PAROLLES The duke knows him for no other but a poor officer of mine,   165
    and writ to me this other day to turn him out a'th'band. I think
    I have his letter in my pocket.

INTERPRETER Marry, we'll search.

PAROLLES In good sadness, I do not know. Either it is there, or it is
    upon a file with the duke's other letters in my tent.   170

INTERPRETER Here 'tis, here's a paper. Shall I read it to you?

PAROLLES I do not know if it be it or no.

BERTRAM Our interpreter does it well.

FIRST LORD Excellently.

INTERPRETER [*Reads*] 'Dian, the count's a fool, and full of gold' –   175

PAROLLES That is not the duke's letter, sir; that is an advertisement
    to a proper maid in Florence, one Diana, to take heed of the
    allurement of one Count Rossillion, a foolish idle boy, but for all
    that very ruttish. I pray you, sir, put it up again.

INTERPRETER Nay, I'll read it first, by your favour.   180

PAROLLES My meaning in't, I protest, was very honest in the behalf
    of the maid; for I knew the young count to be a dangerous and
    lascivious boy, who is a whale to virginity, and devours up all the
    fry it finds.

BERTRAM Damnable both-sides rogue!   185

INTERPRETER [*Reads the*] letter
    'When he swears oaths, bid him drop gold, and take it;
    After he scores, he never pays the score.
    Half won is match well made; match, and well make it;
    He ne'er pays after-debts, take it before,
    And say a soldier, Dian, told thee this: 190
    Men are to mell with, boys are not to kiss;
    For count of this, the count's a fool, I know it,
    Who pays before, but not when he does owe it.
                Thine, as he vowed to thee in thine ear,
                         Parolles.'   195

BERTRAM He shall be whipped through the army with this rhyme in's
    forehead.

Parolles says he wants to live so that he can repent of his misdeeds. He gives more invented details about the dreadful behaviour of the First Lord Dumaine.

1 The wicked Captain Dumaine (a whole class activity)

a 'An egg out of a cloister'

Parolles says Dumaine would steal the most trivial item from the most holy place. He is as immoral as Nessus, who tried to rape the wife of Hercules (a mythological hero of great strength). He would even sell his hope of eternal salvation and his heirs' hopes, too, for the smallest sum of money. Divide into small groups. Each group prepares a very short presentation of one of Captain Dumaine's supposed actions (lines 212–37). Ensure that each group chooses a different action. Present all your ideas in sequence.

b 'I begin to love him for this'

Talk about why Captain Dumaine gives this reaction (line 221) to the list of his supposed dishonourable behaviour. Perhaps it is humorous disbelief at the cheek of Parolles. Perhaps it gives a hint of future mercy for him. Why do you think Dumaine's response is so different from Bertram's?

2 'What say you?' (in small groups)

Why do you think Parolles is so extreme in his damnation of Captain Dumaine? Is it revenge for the way he has been treated? A wish to punish his betters? Is Parolles a social climber? Is he simply trying to save his life? Some other reason?

---

manifold linguist speaker of many languages
armipotent mighty
fain obliged
drum (to announce actors)
tragedians actors
Mile-end a place in London where basic military training took place

doubling of files a very simple military drill
the rarity his unmatchable performance
cardecue French coin of very low value
fee-simple eternal possession

SECOND LORD This is your devoted friend, sir, the manifold linguist
    and the armipotent soldier.
BERTRAM I could endure anything before but a cat, and now he's a cat   200
    to me.
INTERPRETER I perceive, sir, by the general's looks, we shall be fain
    to hang you.
PAROLLES My life, sir, in any case! Not that I am afraid to die, but
    that my offences being many, I would repent out the remainder of   205
    my nature. Let me live, sir, in a dungeon, i'th'stocks, or anywhere,
    so I may live.
INTERPRETER We'll see what may be done, so you confess freely;
    therefore once more to this Captain Dumaine. You have answered
    to his reputation with the duke, and to his valour. What is his   210
    honesty?
PAROLLES He will steal, sir, an egg out of a cloister. For rapes and
    ravishments he parallels Nessus. He professes not keeping of oaths;
    in breaking 'em he is stronger than Hercules. He will lie, sir, with
    such volubility, that you would think truth were a fool. Drunkenness   215
    is his best virtue, for he will be swine-drunk, and in his sleep he
    does little harm, save to his bed-clothes about him; but they know
    his conditions, and lay him in straw. I have but little more to say,
    sir, of his honesty. He has everything that an honest man should
    not have; what an honest man should have, he has nothing.   220
FIRST LORD I begin to love him for this.
BERTRAM For this description of thine honesty? A pox upon him for
    me, he's more and more a cat.
INTERPRETER What say you to his expertness in war?
PAROLLES Faith, sir, h'as led the drum before the English tragedians.   225
    To belie him I will not, and more of his soldiership I know not,
    except in that country he had the honour to be the officer at a place
    there called Mile-end, to instruct for the doubling of files. I would
    do the man what honour I can, but of this I am not certain.
FIRST LORD He hath out-villained villainy so far, that the rarity   230
    redeems him.
BERTRAM A pox on him, he's a cat still.
INTERPRETER His qualities being at this poor price, I need not to ask
    you if gold will corrupt him to revolt.
PAROLLES Sir, for a cardecue he will sell the fee-simple of his   235
    salvation, the inheritance of it, and cut th'entail from all remainders,
    and a perpetual succession for it perpetually.

Parolles says the Second Lord is an evil coward. Parolles is condemned to death for betraying his comrades. His blindfold is removed. He is silent as he sees that his captors are his own fellow soldiers.

1 'Let me see my death!' (in small groups)

a The 'gulling' scene is both funny and painful. Talk together about the way in which the humour sharpens the serious points.

b Decide how you feel Parolles would behave at his 'unmuffling'.

2 Exeunt (in large groups)

Make as much as you can of the simple stage direction at line 269. Individually, work out how you will show your feelings towards Parolles as you leave him, then come together to present the moment.

---

lackey servant
coming on advancing in battle
beguile the supposition of delude
discovered revealed
pestiferous pernicious
am for am off to

And if
but women were there were only
women who
begin . . . nation father a
shameless people

INTERPRETER What's his brother, the other Captain Dumaine?

SECOND LORD Why does he ask him of me?

INTERPRETER What's he?   240

PAROLLES E'en a crow a'th'same nest; not altogether so great as the
first in goodness, but greater a great deal in evil. He excels his
brother for a coward, yet his brother is reputed one of the best that
is. In a retreat he outruns any lackey; marry, in coming on he has
the cramp.   245

INTERPRETER If your life be saved, will you undertake to betray the
Florentine?

PAROLLES Ay, and the captain of his horse, Count Rossillion.

INTERPRETER I'll whisper with the general, and know his pleasure.

PAROLLES I'll no more drumming, a plague of all drums! Only to seem   250
to deserve well, and to beguile the supposition of that lascivious
young boy the count, have I run into this danger. Yet who would
have suspected an ambush where I was taken?

INTERPRETER There is no remedy, sir, but you must die. The general
says, you that have so traitorously discovered the secrets of your   255
army, and made such pestiferous reports of men very nobly held,
can serve the world for no honest use; therefore you must die.
Come, headsman, off with his head.

PAROLLES O Lord, sir, let me live, or let me see my death!

INTERPRETER That shall you, and take your leave of all your friends.   260
                    [*Unmuffling him*]
So, look about you. Know you any here?

BERTRAM Good morrow, noble captain.

SECOND LORD God bless you, Captain Parolles.

FIRST LORD God save you, noble captain.

SECOND LORD Captain, what greeting will you to my Lord Lafew? I   265
am for France.

FIRST LORD Good captain, will you give me a copy of the sonnet you
writ to Diana in behalf of the Count Rossillion? And I were not
a very coward, I'd compel it of you, but fare you well.
                              Exeunt [Bertram and Lords]

INTERPRETER You are undone, captain, all but your scarf; that has a   270
knot on't yet.

PAROLLES Who cannot be crushed with a plot?

INTERPRETER If you could find out a country where but women were
that had received so much shame, you might begin an impudent
nation. Fare ye well, sir, I am for France too. We shall speak of   275
you there.   *Exit [with Soldiers]*

Parolles resolves to survive – comfortably! In Scene 4, Helena tells the Widow that they will go to Marseilles to seek the King's support, then return home. Bertram is on his way home, believing Helena dead.

1 'Simply the thing I am/Shall make me live' (in pairs)

a List the qualities Parolles has which will help him survive. What do you think he will do next?

b Talk together about whether or not you think these lines contain any profound truths. Think of people you know who have survived bad times because of their own efforts and their personal qualities.

2 A soliloquy in verse

a Parolles' speech is one of several soliloquies in the play. What different ways are there of delivering it, apart from speaking directly to the audience? (Read page 12 for some suggestions.)

b Parolles has spoken in prose for the whole of Scene 3. He changes to verse for his soliloquy. Why? Your reasons may give you some help as to how you want to act the soliloquy.

3 The final stages of Helena's plan

In the first fourteen lines of Scene 4 there are reminders of Helena's cure of the King and of his gratitude, and of Bertram's vow not to return to France as long as Helena is living there. What do you expect Helena to do once she returns to Rossillion? Check your predictions as you read on.

---

surety guarantee
pèrfect mine intents achieve my goal
flinty Tartar's bosom warrior's hard heart

His grace his majesty the King
convenient convoy suitable transport
breaking disbanding

PAROLLES Yet am I thankful. If my heart were great,
    'Twould burst at this. Captain I'll be no more,
    But I will eat, and drink, and sleep as soft
    As captain shall. Simply the thing I am   280
    Shall make me live. Who knows himself a braggart,
    Let him fear this; for it will come to pass
    That every braggart shall be found an ass.
    Rust sword, cool blushes, and, Parolles, live
    Safest in shame! Being fooled, by fool'ry thrive!   285
    There's place and means for every man alive.
    I'll after them.   *Exit*

ACT 4   SCENE 4
Florence   The Widow's lodging

Enter HELENA, *the* WIDOW *and* DIANA

HELENA That you may well perceive I have not wronged you,
    One of the greatest in the Christian world
    Shall be my surety; 'fore whose throne 'tis needful,
    Ere I can pèrfect mine intents, to kneel.
    Time was, I did him a desirèd office,   5
    Dear almost as his life, which gratitude
    Through flinty Tartar's bosom would peep forth,
    And answer thanks. I duly am informed
    His grace is at Marseilles, to which place
    We have convenient convoy. You must know   10
    I am supposèd dead. The army breaking,
    My husband hies him home, where heaven aiding,
    And by the leave of my good lord the king,
    We'll be before our welcome.
WIDOW   Gentle madam,
    You never had a servant to whose trust   15
    Your business was more welcome,

Helena will repay her friends' help. She wonders at the way Bertram's lust has helped to trick him. She has another task for Diana. In Scene 5, Lafew says that Parolles misled Bertram. The Countess mourns Helena.

1 Strength in friendship

There are few women in the play. In Act 1, the Countess supports Helena's wish to go to court. Later, Helena needs the help of two women to regain her husband. Think of other situations where women need to band together to resist the power of men. The suffragettes are one historical example. Do you think women still fight today?

2 Strange and sweet (in pairs)

a Helena remembers her hour with Bertram in lines 21–5. Read them aloud. Then identify all the adjectives in the lines and talk together about what these words tell you about her feelings. Suggest what Helena might have said had she not paused at the end of line 25.

b Sophie Thompson (Helena in the 1992 Royal Shakespeare Company production) said she felt this memory was so intimate that the lines should be spoken as a soliloquy or an aside. What effect would such a delivery have?

3 'All's well that ends well' (in small groups)

Once again the image of the rose is used ('briers' and 'thorns', line 32). Helena has suffered the 'thorns' of love, and now expects the sweetness of the 'leaves' (petals). After the barrenness of winter, comes the reward of summer – 'All's well that ends well'. Helena hopes to achieve her aim of gaining Bertram as a husband in more than name. Talk about whether you think her suffering will have been worthwhile.

---

dower dowry
motive agent
saucy . . . thoughts lustful
acceptance of deceived feelings
for that which is away thinking it
to be someone who is elsewhere

the fine's the result is
renown reward
saffron yellow dye for clothes or
cooking (the colour of cowards)

HELENA   Nor you, mistress,
        Ever a friend whose thoughts more truly labour
        To recompense your love. Doubt not but heaven
        Hath brought me up to be your daughter's dower,
        As it hath fated her to be my motive   20
        And helper to a husband. But O, strange men,
        That can such sweet use make of what they hate,
        When saucy trusting of the cozened thoughts
        Defiles the pitchy night; so lust doth play
        With what it loathes for that which is away –   25
        But more of this hereafter. You, Diana,
        Under my poor instructions yet must suffer
        Something in my behalf.
DIANA   Let death and honesty
        Go with your impositions, I am yours
        Upon your will to suffer.
HELENA   Yet, I pray you: 30
        But with the word the time will bring on summer,
        When briers shall have leaves as well as thorns,
        And be as sweet as sharp. We must away:
        Our wagon is prepared, and time revives us.
        All's well that ends well; still the fine's the crown.   35
        Whate'er the course, the end is the renown.

                                                    Exeunt

ACT 4   SCENE 5
The Palace of Rossillion

Enter the COUNTESS, LAVATCH and Lord LAFEW

LAFEW No, no, no, your son was misled with a snipped-taffeta fellow
    there, whose villainous saffron would have made all the unbaked
    and doughy youth of a nation in his colour. Your daughter-in-law
    had been alive at this hour, and your son here at home, more
    advanced by the king than by that red-tailed humble-bee I speak   5
    of.
COUNTESS I would I had not known him; it was the death of the most
    virtuous gentlewoman that ever nature had praise for creating. If
    she had partaken of my flesh, and cost me the dearest groans of a
    mother, I could not have owed her a more rooted love.   10

Lavatch and Lafew praise Helena, then exchange puns. Lavatch continues his talk of serving the devil. His story is too long to keep Lafew's interest.

---

1 'And I would give his wife my bauble, sir, to do her service'

Lavatch attempts a genuine compliment to Helena but soon reverts to his usual sexual innuendo: 'service' is a pun on sexual intercourse; 'fisnomy is more hotter in France' means that his face (physiognomy) is hot with the symptoms of syphilis, the 'French disease'.

Work in groups of three. Take a part each and act out lines 11–48. Concentrate on Lafew's reactions. How amused is he? As the Countess is on-stage, he may not wish to show how amused he is. Decide what the Countess is doing during their conversation. She knows Lavatch's ways very well (see lines 50–1 on page 145 for one reason why she keeps him on at the palace). She may indicate to Lafew that the conversation has gone on long enough.

---

sallets salads
herb of grace rue (rue also means 'repent')
nose-herbs fragrant herbs
Nebuchadnezzar King of Babylon, punished by God, who made him eat grass (Elizabethans pronounced 'grass' and 'grace' similarly)

cozen cheat
maine probably a misprint for name
great fire hell
jades' tricks tricks played on/by weary (jaded) horses

LAFEW 'Twas a good lady, 'twas a good lady. We may pick a thousand
sallets ere we light on such another herb.

LAVATCH Indeed, sir, she was the sweet marjoram of the sallet, or rather
the herb of grace.

LAFEW They are not herbs, you knave, they are nose-herbs.   15

LAVATCH I am no great Nebuchadnezzar, sir, I have not much skill in
grace.

LAFEW Whether dost thou profess thyself – a knave or a fool?

LAVATCH A fool, sir, at a woman's service, and a knave at a man's.

LAFEW Your distinction?   20

LAVATCH I would cozen the man of his wife and do his service.

LAFEW So you were a knave at his service indeed.

LAVATCH And I would give his wife my bauble, sir, to do her service.

LAFEW I will subscribe for thee, thou art both knave and fool.

LAVATCH At your service.   25

LAFEW No, no, no.

LAVATCH Why, sir, if I cannot serve you, I can serve as great a prince
as you are.

LAFEW Who's that? A Frenchman?

LAVATCH Faith, sir, 'a has an English maine, but his fisnomy is more   30
hotter in France than there.

LAFEW What prince is that?

LAVATCH The black prince, sir, alias the prince of darkness, alias the
devil.

LAFEW Hold thee, there's my purse. I give thee not this to suggest thee   35
from thy master thou talk'st of; serve him still.

LAVATCH I am a woodland fellow, sir, that always loved a great fire,
and the master I speak of ever keeps a good fire. But sure he is the
prince of the world; let his nobility remain in's court. I am for the
house with the narrow gate, which I take to be too little for pomp   40
to enter. Some that humble themselves may, but the many will be
too chill and tender, and they'll be for the flowery way that leads
to the broad gate and the great fire.

LAFEW Go thy ways, I begin to be aweary of thee, and I tell thee so
before, because I would not fall out with thee. Go thy ways, let my   45
horses be well looked to, without any tricks.

LAVATCH If I put any tricks upon 'em, sir, they shall be jades' tricks,
which are their own right by the law of nature.   *Exit*

Lafew wants his daughter to marry Bertram. He has the King's permission. The Countess is pleased to agree. The King is expected next day, Bertram that night. Lavatch announces Bertram's arrival.

1 Who are you talking about? (in groups of six)

This activity will help you understand the script opposite. Spread out into a circle. Each person takes a part (Lavatch, Lafew, the Countess, the late Count, Helena, Bertram). Read the page aloud, pointing to each character as he or she is mentioned in the script. The technical name for this activity is 'deixis'. You will find the technique helpful for other parts of the script.

2 Bertram's wife

Lines 56–7 suggest that the notion of Bertram marrying Lafew's daughter is an old idea revived. List possible reasons why Lafew wants Bertram for a son-in-law.

3 The patch of velvet

The patch would be covering a wound. It could be an injury received honourably in battle, or an incision ('carbonado') made to relieve the disease syphilis. In the 1992 Royal Shakespeare Company production, Bertram's 'patch' was heavy stubble where he had found it too painful to shave over an injury. Which of these three versions would you use in a production? Each possibility gives a different slant on Bertram's character.

Notice that Lavatch has invented a new quality of fabric for his joke about the thickness of the bandage – 'two pile and a half'. Velvet was graded according to thickness, three pile being the thickest.

---

shrewd bitter
unhappy hurtful
made himself . . . out of him took great pleasure in his company
patent licence
has no pace cannot be reined in

post speedily
made . . . charter put forward my request too boldly
carbonadoed slashed (a way of preparing meat for boiling)

LAFEW A shrewd knave and an unhappy.

COUNTESS So 'a is. My lord that's gone made himself much sport out   50
of him. By his authority he remains here, which he thinks is a patent
for his sauciness, and indeed he has no pace, but runs where he
will.

LAFEW I like him well, 'tis not amiss. And I was about to tell you, since
I heard of the good lady's death, and that my lord your son was   55
upon his return home, I moved the king my master to speak in the
behalf of my daughter, which in the minority of them both, his
majesty, out of a self-gracious remembrance, did first propose. His
highness hath promised me to do it, and to stop up the displeasure
he hath conceived against your son, there is no fitter matter. How   60
does your ladyship like it?

COUNTESS With very much content, my lord, and I wish it happily
effected.

LAFEW His highness comes post from Marseilles, of as able body as
when he numbered thirty. 'A will be here tomorrow, or I am   65
deceived by him that in such intelligence hath seldom failed.

COUNTESS It rejoices me, that I hope I shall see him ere I die. I have
letters that my son will be here tonight. I shall beseech your
lordship to remain with me till they meet together.

LAFEW Madam, I was thinking with what manners I might safely be   70
admitted.

COUNTESS You need but plead your honourable privilege.

LAFEW Lady, of that I have made a bold charter, but I thank my God
it holds yet.

Enter [LAVATCH, *the*] *Clown*

LAVATCH O madam, yonder's my lord your son with a patch of velvet   75
on's face. Whether there be a scar under't or no, the velvet knows,
but 'tis a goodly patch of velvet. His left cheek is a cheek of two
pile and a half, but his right cheek is worn bare.

LAFEW A scar nobly got, or a noble scar, is a good livery of honour;
so belike is that.   80

LAVATCH But it is your carbonadoed face.

LAFEW Let us go see your son, I pray you. I long to talk with the young
noble soldier.

LAVATCH Faith, there's a dozen of 'em, with delicate fine hats, and most
courteous feathers, which bow the head, and nod at every man.   85

Exeunt

Looking back at Act 4
Activities for groups and individuals

1 'Good and ill together'

Do you think the First Lord's words about human character in Act 4 Scene 3, lines 60–3, fit all the characters in *All's Well*? Work through the cast list on page 1. Consider each character in turn, and decide whether there is anyone either wholly good or wholly bad.

2 'Hoodman comes!'

a Think about Parolles' entrance for his interrogation (Act 4 Scene 3, line 99). If you were directing the play, how would you want your designer to costume Parolles? He has been in the stocks all night. Would you want him to look as though some additional punishment has been carried out? This production photograph shows one way of answering the question.

b Read Scene 3, lines 154–247. Stage the extract, concentrating on the reactions of the victims as each is ridiculed by Parolles.

c Present a series of tableaux to show the decline of Parolles in Act 4 Scenes 1 and 3, from the braggart to the conquered. One person speaks a line from the script as a caption for each 'snapshot'.

3 Fortune

There are references throughout the play to the influence of the stars on people's lives. Many Elizabethans saw Fortune as a fickle woman, or as a wheel on which your position was never secure.

Do you find it believable that Helena has to use extreme methods (the 'bed trick') to break out of the restrictions of Fate? Or do you think Shakespeare is simply using a convenient device to end the play?

The wheel of Fortune.   Fortune-telling.

4 The bed trick

The 'bed trick' is quite a common device in sixteenth- and seventeenth-century plays. One woman agrees to sleep with a man, but another woman takes her place. Since the trick takes place in the dark, and the woman does not speak, the man is unaware of the swap.

In *Measure for Measure*, Angelo, the Duke of Vienna's deputy, has been left in command in the Duke's absence. He revives old laws against sexual immorality and condemns Claudio to death for getting his fiancée pregnant. Claudio's sister Isabella, a novice nun, pleads with Angelo for her brother's life. Angelo tells her that if she sleeps with him, he will save Claudio. She initially refuses, but is persuaded to pretend to agree. The substitute in this bed trick will be Mariana, Angelo's former fiancée.

Helena assures Diana and the Widow that she is eternally in their debt.
They ask a gentleman falconer to take a message to the King, but he tells
them that the King has already left.

The Gentle Astringer is a strange character. He has not been seen before, and nothing in the plot prepares for his entry. The character is named as 'a Gentle Astringer' in the First Folio copy of the plays (see page 188). Because there is nothing in the script about his profession ('astringer' means 'falconer'), some editors assume that Shakespeare's handwriting was misread. In some editions he is called a 'gentle stranger'. How would you explain such an unexpected character turning up at this point in the play?

exceeding posting fast travelling
bold confident
requital obligation to repay you
goes upon speaks of

goaded . . . occasions impelled by urgent reasons
nice manners politeness
virtues powers

ACT 5   SCENE 1
Marseilles

Enter HELENA *the* WIDOW, DIANA *and attendants*

HELENA But this exceeding posting day and night
Must wear your spirits low; we cannot help it.
But since you have made the days and nights as one,
To wear your gentle limbs in my affairs,
Be bold you do so grow in my requital   5
As nothing can unroot you.

Enter [GENTLEMAN,] *a* GENTLE ASTRINGER

                                    In happy time!
This man may help me to his majesty's ear,
If he would spend his power. God save you, sir.
GENTLEMAN And you.
HELENA Sir, I have seen you in the court of France.   10
GENTLEMAN I have been sometimes there.
HELENA I do presume, sir, that you are not fall'n
From the report that goes upon your goodness,
And therefore goaded with most sharp occasions,
Which lay nice manners by, I put you to   15
The use of your own virtues, for the which
I shall continue thankful.
GENTLEMAN   What's your will?
HELENA That it will please you
To give this poor petition to the king,
And aid me with that store of power you have   20
To come into his presence.
GENTLEMAN The king's not here.
HELENA   Not here, sir?
GENTLEMAN   Not indeed.
He hence removed last night, and with more haste
Than is his use.
WIDOW   Lord, how we lose our pains!

The gentleman falconer reports that the King has gone to Rossillion. He agrees to take Helena's message. She says she will follow more slowly. In Scene 2, Lavatch complains that Parolles stinks.

1 'All's well that ends well yet' (in pairs)

Line 25 is the second time that Helena has echoed the title of the play. The first time was as she set off from Florence in Act 4 Scene 4. What do you think is Helena's mood here? How would you want her to say the line to convey her emotions to an audience?

2 'Go, go, provide' (in groups of six to eight)

To whom is line 38 addressed:

● to a group of servants on-stage – or off?
● to the Widow and Diana? (Would the line sound arrogant?)
● to the Gentle Astringer?

Try out different tableaux for the line. Presumably the three women are all very tired and disappointed not to have found the King after their long journey. Do you think a crowded stage is more effective at this point, or a relatively empty one?

3 Parolles' journey

Lines 1–15 suggest that Parolles' journey from Italy has been difficult and uncomfortable. He is dishevelled and he smells! Write an imaginary account of his travels which gives reasons for his present condition.

---

what good . . . means as fast as our resources will permit
allow the wind stand downwind (so I can't smell you)

close-stool small cupboard containing a chamber-pot (namely, a toilet)

HELENA All's well that ends well yet,   25
            Though time seem so adverse and means unfit.
            I do beseech you, whither is he gone?
GENTLEMAN Marry, as I take it, to Rossillion,
            Whither I am going.
HELENA   I do beseech you, sir,
            Since you are like to see the king before me,   30
            Commend the paper to his gracious hand,
            Which I presume shall render you no blame,
            But rather make you thank your pains for it.
            I will come after you with what good speed
            Our means will make us means.
GENTLEMAN   This I'll do for you.   35
HELENA And you shall find yourself to be well thanked,
            Whate'er falls more. We must to horse again.
            Go, go, provide.
                                                              [*Exeunt*]

ACT 5   SCENE 2
The Palace of Rossillion

Enter LAVATCH and PAROLLES

PAROLLES Good Master Lavatch, give my Lord Lafew this letter. I
    have ere now, sir, been better known to you, when I have held
    familiarity with fresher clothes; but I am now, sir, muddied in
    Fortune's mood, and smell somewhat strong of her strong
    displeasure.   5
LAVATCH Truly, Fortune's displeasure is but sluttish if it smell so
    strongly as thou speak'st of. I will henceforth eat no fish of
    Fortune's buttering. Prithee allow the wind.
PAROLLES Nay, you need not to stop your nose, sir; I spake but by
    a metaphor.   10
LAVATCH Indeed, sir, if your metaphor stink, I will stop my nose, or
    against any man's metaphor. Prithee get thee further.
PAROLLES Pray you, sir, deliver me this paper.
LAVATCH Foh, prithee stand away. A paper from Fortune's close-stool
    to give to a nobleman! Look here he comes himself.   15

Parolles asks for help from Lafew, who gives him money. Parolles says that Lafew was the first to discover his faults. Lafew agrees to help him.

A changed Parolles. Compare this picture of Parolles with those on page 104.

not a musk-cat not sweet-smelling (perfume was made from secretions of musk deer and civet cats)
withal with it
ingenious stupid
cardecue small French coin
justices justices of the peace

'word' (Lafew is joking about Parolles' name meaning 'words')
Cox my passion! by God's suffering! (a mild oath)
found me found me out
bring me in some grace bring me into favour

Enter LAFEW

Here is a purr of Fortune's, sir, or of Fortune's cat – but not a
musk-cat – that has fall'n into the unclean fishpond of her
displeasure, and as he says, is muddied withal. Pray you, sir, use
the carp as you may, for he looks like a poor, decayed, ingenious,
foolish, rascally knave. I do pity his distress in my similes of comfort,   20
and leave him to your lordship.   [*Exit*]

PAROLLES My lord, I am a man whom Fortune hath cruelly scratched.

LAFEW And what would you have me to do? 'Tis too late to pare her
nails now. Wherein have you played the knave with Fortune that
she should scratch you, who of herself is a good lady, and would   25
not have knaves thrive long under her? There's a cardecue for you.
Let the justices make you and Fortune friends; I am for other
business.

PAROLLES I beseech your honour to hear me one single word.

LAFEW You beg a single penny more. Come, you shall ha't; save your   30
word.

PAROLLES My name, my good lord, is Parolles.

LAFEW You beg more than 'word' then. Cox my passion! give me your
hand. How does your drum?

PAROLLES O my good lord, you were the first that found me!   35

LAFEW Was I, in sooth? And I was the first that lost thee.

PAROLLES It lies in you, my lord, to bring me in some grace, for you
did bring me out.

LAFEW Out upon thee, knave! Dost thou put upon me at once both the
office of God and the devil? One brings thee in grace, and the other   40
brings thee out.

[*Trumpets sound*]

The king's coming, I know by his trumpets. Sirrah, enquire further
after me. I had talk of you last night; though you are a fool and
a knave, you shall eat. Go to, follow.

PAROLLES I praise God for you.   45

[*Exeunt*]

The King speaks of his grief for the death of Helena and blames Bertram for not valuing her. The Countess begs forgiveness for Bertram and the King pardons him. Lafew praises Helena.

1 Forgiveness (in groups of three)

a Take parts and read lines 1–27 two or three times. Write down your character's feelings in a single sentence. Discuss whether you feel you have all focused precisely on the characters' different attitudes towards Bertram and Helena.

b In role, debate whether or not Bertram should be forgiven. Bear in mind your character's limited knowledge about Bertram's activities in Florence – you know that he has been heroic, but you don't know about Diana.

c Out of role, debate the issue again using your own more complete knowledge of the play so far.

2 A jewel (in pairs)

The King says 'Praising what is lost/Makes the remembrance dear' (lines 19–20). This adage reflects other similar sayings, such as 'absence makes the heart grow fonder'. Talk together about whether these sayings reflect your own experience, or whether 'out of sight, out of mind' is more relevant. Find echoes of this last proverb in lines 24–5. Improvise a short dialogue which incorporates both points of view.

---

our esteem my worth
estimation home true worth
Natural rebellion rebellion of the natural passions
i'th'blade in the immaturity

watched the time waited for
Th'incensing relics the reminders which arouse anger
A stranger someone whose past is not known

ACT 5   SCENE 3
The Palace of Rossillion

Trumpet and fanfare   Enter the KING, *the* COUNTESS, LAFEW, *the*
FIRST *and* SECOND LORDS *Dumaine and attendants*

KING We lost a jewel of her, and our esteem
        Was made much poorer by it; but your son,
        As mad in folly, lacked the sense to know
        Her estimation home.
COUNTESS   'Tis past, my liege,
        And I beseech your majesty to make it   5
        Natural rebellion, done i'th'blade of youth,
        When oil and fire, too strong for reason's force,
        O'erbears it, and burns on.
KING   My honoured lady,
        I have forgiven and forgotten all,
        Though my revenges were high bent upon him,   10
        And watched the time to shoot.
LAFEW   This I must say –
        But first I beg my pardon – the young lord
        Did to his majesty, his mother, and his lady
        Offence of mighty note; but to himself
        The greatest wrong of all. He lost a wife   15
        Whose beauty did astonish the survey
        Of richest eyes, whose words all ears took captive,
        Whose dear perfection hearts that scorned to serve
        Humbly called mistress.
KING   Praising what is lost
        Makes the remembrance dear. Well, call him hither,   20
        We are reconciled, and the first view shall kill
        All repetition. Let him not ask our pardon,
        The nature of his great offence is dead,
        And deeper than oblivion we do bury
        Th'incensing relics of it. Let him approach   25
        A stranger, no offender; and inform him
        So 'tis our will he should.
GENTLEMAN   I shall, my liege.   *[Exit]*

Lafew and the King discuss Bertram's possible marriage to Lafew's daughter. Bertram enters and asks for the King's forgiveness. He says his first choice was Lafew's daughter, and declares he loved Helena.

1 Bertram's excuses (in pairs)

a Critics are undecided about the precise meaning of Bertram's lines 44–9. The fact that he is finding it difficult to express himself clearly suggests quite a lot about his feelings at this moment.

Do you think he is saying: 'I liked Maudlin (Lafew's daughter) first, but before I had the courage to say so, contempt for Helena made every woman seem hideous.' Or is he saying: 'I liked Maudlin first, before I rashly defied the King, and it was because I loved her that I thought Helena was hideous.'

Talk about which interpretation you think is more likely, and about what you think is Bertram's state of mind as he speaks these lines.

b Read through lines 44–54 once or twice. Talk together about the excuses Bertram is making, and whether or not you believe them. Then, with one of you as Bertram and the other as his *alter ego*, read the lines again with Bertram pausing at the punctuation marks, so that his *alter ego* can express his meaning in blunt, modern English.

2 'Well excused'

How does the King say line 55? Ironically . . . approvingly . . . sarcastically . . . doubtfully . . . or . . . ? If you were playing the King, what would you want the audience to understand about your feelings at this point in the play?

---

hath reference to is at the disposal of

not a day of season not in one single mood

Distracted broken

blames sins

take the instant by the forward top seize the opportunity

ere my heart . . . tongue before I dared speak what was in my heart

Where . . . infixing where my eye fixed its impressions (on my heart)

favour face

Extended or contracted distorted

scores debts

compt account

KING What says he to your daughter? Have you spoke?
LAFEW All that he is hath reference to your highness.
KING Then shall we have a match. I have letters sent me   30
      That sets him high in fame.

            Enter COUNT BERTRAM

LAFEW   He looks well on't.
KING I am not a day of season,
      For thou mayst see a sunshine and a hail
      In me at once. But to the brightest beams
      Distracted clouds give way, so stand thou forth,   35
      The time is fair again.
BERTRAM   My high-repented blames,
      Dear sovereign, pardon to me.
KING   All is whole,
      Not one word more of the consumèd time.
      Let's take the instant by the forward top;
      For we are old, and on our quick'st decrees   40
      Th'inaudible and noiseless foot of time
      Steals ere we can effect them. You remember
      The daughter of this lord?
BERTRAM Admiringly, my liege. At first
      I stuck my choice upon her, ere my heart   45
      Durst make too bold a herald of my tongue;
      Where the impression of mine eye infixing,
      Contempt his scornful pèrspective did lend me,
      Which warped the line of every other favour,
      Scorned a fair colour, or expressed it stol'n,   50
      Extended or contracted all proportions
      To a most hideous object. Thence it came
      That she whom all men praised, and whom myself,
      Since I have lost, have loved, was in mine eye
      The dust that did offend it.
KING   Well excused.   55
      That thou didst love her, strikes some scores away
      From the great compt; but love that comes too late,
      Like a remorseful pardon slowly carried,
      To the great sender turns a sour offence,
      Crying, 'That's good that's gone.' Our rash faults   60
      Make trivial price of serious things we have,
      Not knowing them until we know their grave.

The King instructs Bertram to forget Helena and send a love token to Lafew's daughter. Bertram offers his ring. Lafew, the King and the Countess all claim it is the one given to Helena by the King. Bertram denies it.

1 Regretting what's done (in small groups)

The King's lines 63–6 refer to a common human failing: regretting something when it is too late. Improvise a short scene where one character deeply regrets something he or she has done, or not done, earlier.

2 'Be this sweet Helen's knell' (in pairs)

A knell is a funeral bell, so in line 67 the King is symbolically 'burying' Helena. He tells Bertram 'now forget her'. Talk about what you think of the matter-of-fact way in which she is dismissed by the King. Do you think it is a typically male response?

3 The 'fair Maudlin'

This is the only time Lafew's daughter is mentioned by name. Would you want her to appear in your production (in Act 2, perhaps)? Write a soliloquy for her which makes clear her feelings for Bertram.

4 The ring (in groups of four)

a Talk together about how Bertram feels when first Lafew, then the King, then his mother comment on the ring.

b What actually happens to the ring on-stage? Decide whether you would want to use an obviously unusual ring in your production. Read lines 73–92 focusing on the ring and how it is passed around on-stage. Who is holding the ring at line 90?

The main . . . had all parties are agreed
Or, ere . . . cesse! if Bertram's second marriage is going to match his first, the Countess hopes she will die

digested absorbed
favour token
relieve assist
reave rob
stead aid

Oft our displeasures, to ourselves unjust,
Destroy our friends, and after weep their dust;
Our own love waking cries to see what's done, 65
While shameful hate sleeps out the afternoon.
Be this sweet Helen's knell, and now forget her.
Send forth your amorous token for fair Maudlin.
The main consents are had, and here we'll stay
To see our widower's second marriage day. 70

COUNTESS Which better than the first, O dear heaven, bless!
Or, ere they meet, in me, O nature, cesse!

LAFEW Come on, my son, in whom my house's name
Must be digested; give a favour from you
To sparkle in the spirits of my daughter, 75
That she may quickly come.

[*Bertram gives a ring*]

By my old beard,
And every hair that's on't, Helen, that's dead,
Was a sweet creature; such a ring as this,
The last that e'er I took her leave at court,
I saw upon her finger.

BERTRAM   Hers it was not. 80

KING Now pray you let me see it; for mine eye,
While I was speaking, oft was fastened to't.
This ring was mine, and when I gave it Helen,
I bade her, if her fortunes ever stood
Necessitied to help, that by this token 85
I would relieve her. Had you that craft to reave her
Of what should stead her most?

BERTRAM   My gracious sovereign,
Howe'er it pleases you to take it so,
The ring was never hers.

COUNTESS   Son, on my life,
I have seen her wear it, and she reckoned it 90
At her life's rate.

LAFEW   I am sure I saw her wear it.

159

Bertram protests that the ring was thrown to him in Florence by a noble lady who was in love with him. The King does not believe his story, and has Bertram arrested.

1 Quick wits or self-preservation?

If you were directing Bertram in this scene, how would you advise him to say lines 92–101? Hesitantly . . . confidently . . . abruptly . . . defiantly . . . ? Remember, Bertram has to make a case to the King, who has it in his power to arrest him on the spot (which he does).

How would you advise the actor to speak lines 112 and 124–7 to be consistent with your ideas about Bertram's character?

2 'This ring was mine' (in pairs)

The scene described in lines 108–12 (and lines 83–6 on the previous page) does not appear in the play. Write the dialogue for the missing scene and perform it for the class.

3 'Tinct and multiplying med'cine'

Plutus was the Greek god of wealth. The Elizabethans were obsessed by alchemy and the search for the Philosopher's Stone which would change base metal into gold and produce the elixir of life. In lines 101–4, the King is saying that he knows more about the ring than Plutus knew about the mystery of the Philosopher's Stone. Suggest the tone in which he speaks the lines.

---

ingaged promised to her
subscribed . . . fortune told her my situation
ceased . . . satisfaction regretfully stopped pursuing me
science intimate knowledge
called . . . surety swore by the saints

Upon . . . disaster when she was in great trouble
fain desire to
My fore-past proofs evidence I already had
tax . . . vanity reproach my fear for being too weak

BERTRAM You are deceived, my lord, she never saw it.
In Florence was it from a casement thrown me,
Wrapped in a paper, which contained the name
Of her that threw it. Noble she was, and thought   95
I stood ingaged; but when I had subscribed
To mine own fortune, and informed her fully
I could not answer in that course of honour
As she had made the overture, she ceased
In heavy satisfaction, and would never   100
Receive the ring again.
KING   Plutus himself,
That knows the tinct and multiplying med'cine,
Hath not in nature's mystery more science
Than I have in this ring. 'Twas mine, 'twas Helen's,
Whoever gave it you. Then if you know   105
That you are well acquainted with yourself,
Confess 'twas hers, and by what rough enforcement
You got it from her. She called the saints to surety
That she would never put it from her finger,
Unless she gave it to yourself in bed,   110
Where you have never come, or sent it us
Upon her great disaster.
BERTRAM   She never saw it.
KING Thou speak'st it falsely, as I love mine honour,
And mak'st conjectural fears to come into me,
Which I would fain shut out. If it should prove   115
That thou art so inhuman – 'twill not prove so;
And yet I know not: thou didst hate her deadly,
And she is dead, which nothing but to close
Her eyes myself could win me to believe,
More than to see this ring. Take him away.   120
My fore-past proofs, howe'er the matter fall,
Shall tax my fears of little vanity,
Having vainly feared too little. Away with him!
We'll sift this matter further.
BERTRAM   If you shall prove
This ring was ever hers, you shall as easy   125
Prove that I husbanded her bed in Florence,
Where yet she never was.

                                        [*Exit guarded*]

The Gentle Astringer brings a letter from Diana. She accuses Bertram of seducing her by promising to marry her when his wife died. She claims his hand. Bertram is brought back to face Diana and her mother.

1 'I am wrapped in dismal thinkings' (in pairs)

Talk together about what is in the King's mind as he speaks line 128.

2 The royal progress

When the Gentle Astringer says that Diana has 'for four or five removes come short' (line 131), he is talking of the stages (stopping places) in the King's journey. When the monarch travelled around the country it was called a 'progress'. He or she would stay, with the entire royal household, at the home of a noble subject. Queen Elizabeth I was notorious for her expensive visits, which were an honour, but often a financial disaster, for her hosts. Diana has just missed the King at four or five earlier stopping places.

3 'A poor maid is undone' (in groups of three)

What do you think is Shakespeare's dramatic purpose in having Diana appear here to claim Bertram? Why do you think she persists with the fiction that Bertram slept with her? Check your guesses as you read further.

4 Son-in-law for sale

In line 146, Lafew is suggesting that he could buy a better son-in-law than Bertram at a market. He also says that he would offer Bertram for sale there by paying to have him registered in the toll book as merchandise. Markets in Elizabethan times were just as likely to offer second-rate goods for sale as many of today's markets.

---

removes stages in a royal journey
Vanquished won over
suppliant petitioner
importing visage urgent
  expression

verbal brief spoken message
Derivèd descended
suit request

Enter GENTLEMAN

KING I am wrapped in dismal thinkings.

GENTLEMAN   Gracious sovereign,
      Whether I have been to blame or no, I know not.
      Here's a petition from a Florentine,   130
      Who hath for four or five removes come short
      To tender it herself. I undertook it,
      Vanquished thereto by the fair grace and speech
      Of the poor suppliant, who by this I know
      Is here attending. Her business looks in her   135
      With an importing visage, and she told me,
      In a sweet verbal brief, it did concern
      Your highness with herself.

[KING] [*Reads*] *a letter* 'Upon his many protestations to marry me when
      his wife was dead, I blush to say it, he won me. Now is the Count   140
      Rossillion a widower, his vows are forfeited to me, and my honour's
      paid to him. He stole from Florence, taking no leave, and I follow
      him to his country for justice. Grant it me, O king, in you it best
      lies; otherwise a seducer flourishes, and a poor maid is undone.
                                          Diana Capilet.'   145

LAFEW I will buy me a son-in-law in a fair, and toll for this. I'll none
      of him.

KING The heavens have thought well on thee, Lafew,
      To bring forth this discovery. Seek these suitors.
      Go speedily, and bring again the count.   150
                              [*Exeunt Attendants*]
      I am afear'd the life of Helen, lady,
      Was foully snatched.

COUNTESS   Now, justice on the doers!

Enter BERTRAM [*guarded*]

KING I wonder, sir, since wives are monsters to you,
      And that you fly them as you swear them lordship,
      Yet you desire to marry. What woman's that?   155

Enter WIDOW, DIANA

DIANA I am, my lord, a wretched Florentine,
      Derivèd from the ancient Capilet.
      My suit, as I do understand, you know,
      And therefore know how far I may be pitied.

Bertram admits that he knows Diana and her mother. Diana says he took her virginity and promised to marry her. She produces the ring he gave her. Bertram claims she slept with all the soldiers.

1 Her or me? (in groups of five)

Stand in a circle. Taking one part each, read lines 160–86. As you come to a word which refers to you or to another person, point clearly to the person mentioned. For example: 'I (*point to yourself*) am her (*point to Diana*) mother, sir (*point to King*)'.

2 Diana's riddles (in pairs)

Several of Diana's speeches in Act 5 are in the form of riddles and are sometimes ambiguous.

a Talk together about how Shakespeare makes Diana's lines 168–73 sound different from the blank verse used by the other characters. Then advise Diana how you feel they should be spoken.

b In line 171, Diana makes a reference to the conventional idea that, in marriage, man and wife are one flesh. If you think that she is exaggerating her claim to Bertram, look back at Act 4 Scene 2, line 53 to see what he promised.

3 Sweet words

Bertram seems to reserve his worst phrases for the women he is lying to. What do you think he means by 'a common gamester' (line 186)? How would Diana react to this on-stage?

---

cease die
comes too short is not good enough
fond foolish
ill to friend unfriendly

gain them, win their friendship
impudent shameless
validity worth
Did . . . parallel was without equal
commoner prostitute

WIDOW I am her mother, sir, whose age and honour   160
      Both suffer under this complaint we bring,
      And both shall cease, without your remedy.
KING Come hither, count, do you know these women?
BERTRAM My lord, I neither can nor will deny
      But that I know them. Do they charge me further?   165
DIANA Why do you look so strange upon your wife?
BERTRAM She's none of mine, my lord.
DIANA   If you shall marry,
      You give away this hand, and that is mine;
      You give away heaven's vows, and those are mine;
      You give away myself, which is known mine;   170
      For I by vow am so embodied yours,
      That she which marries you must marry me,
      Either both or none.
LAFEW Your reputation comes too short for my daughter, you are no
      husband for her.   175
BERTRAM My lord, this is a fond and desperate creature,
      Whom sometime I have laughed with. Let your highness
      Lay a more noble thought upon mine honour
      Than for to think that I would sink it here.
KING Sir, for my thoughts, you have them ill to friend   180
      Till your deeds gain them; fairer prove your honour
      Than in my thought it lies.
DIANA   Good my lord,
      Ask him upon his oath, if he does think
      He had not my virginity.
KING What say'st thou to her?
BERTRAM   She's impudent, my lord,   185
      And was a common gamester to the camp.
DIANA He does me wrong, my lord; if I were so,
      He might have bought me at a common price.
      Do not believe him. O, behold this ring,
      Whose high respect and rich validity   190
      Did lack a parallel; yet for all that
      He gave it to a commoner a'th'camp,
      If I be one.

The Countess identifies the family ring. Diana says Parolles will confirm the truth of her accusation. Bertram admits he slept with Diana, but claims she seduced him. She asks him to return her ring.

1 Cornered! (in small groups)

Everyone is ganging up against Bertram. His mother not only recognises the ring, but also recognises the expression on his face (line 193) which tells her he is lying.

a Talk together about the occasions in your past when someone close to you has known that you are lying, just from the look on your face. Do you have any sympathy for Bertram at this moment?

b How does the Countess say her lines 193–7 (for example: accusingly, distraught, aside, hysterically . . . or . . .)?

2 Parolles' disciple (in pairs)

In Act 4 Scene 5, Lafew and the Countess blame Parolles for leading Bertram astray. Read through lines 202–7 two or three times and decide whether you think the lines suggest that Bertram has indeed learned from Parolles.

3 Excuses, excuses (in groups of four)

Read through lines 207–17, changing reader at each punctuation mark. Do this two or three times until you are sure of the sense. Then divide into pairs. One pair lists all the words and phrases which are about Diana's guilt, and the other pair lists all the words and phrases which imply Bertram's innocence. Compare your lists and talk about your attitude to Bertram. Look back at Act 4 Scene 2 and remind yourselves of the truth of the situation.

---

by testament . . . issue left in a will to the heir
spots a'th'world vices
Am I . . . utter he will say anything about me
boarded had sex with
distance how to tease me (or, the difference between our ranks)

angle for try to catch
fancy (line 212) infatuation
insuite unusual
modern ordinary
Subdued me to her rate made me agree to her price
diet insult

COUNTESS   He blushes, and 'tis hit.
          Of six preceding ancestors, that gem,
          Conferred by testament to th'sequent issue,   195
          Hath it been owed and worn. This is his wife,
          That ring's a thousand proofs.
KING   Methought you said
          You saw one here in court could witness it.
DIANA I did, my lord, but loath am to produce
          So bad an instrument. His name's Parolles.   200
LAFEW I saw the man today, if man he be.
KING Find him, and bring him hither.
                                        [*Exit an Attendant*]
BERTRAM   What of him?
          He's quoted for a most perfidious slave,
          With all the spots a'th'world taxed and debauched,
          Whose nature sickens but to speak a truth.   205
          Am I or that or this for what he'll utter,
          That will speak any thing?
KING   She hath that ring of yours.
BERTRAM I think she has. Certain it is I liked her,
          And boarded her i'th'wanton way of youth.
          She knew her distance, and did angle for me,   210
          Madding my eagerness with her restraint,
          As all impediments in fancy's course
          Are motives of more fancy, and in fine,
          Her insuite cunning, with her modern grace,
          Subdued me to her rate. She got the ring,   215
          And I had that which any inferior might
          At market-price have bought.
DIANA   I must be patient.
          You that have turned off a first so noble wife,
          May justly diet me. I pray you yet
          (Since you lack virtue, I will lose a husband)   220
          Send for your ring, I will return it home,
          And give me mine again.
BERTRAM   I have it not.
KING What ring was yours, I pray you?
DIANA   Sir, much like
          The same upon your finger.
KING Know you this ring? This ring was his of late.   225

Diana tells the King that she gave Bertram the ring when they were in bed.
Parolles confirms that Bertram seduced Diana. The King is not pleased by
Parolles' evidence. Diana claims the King's ring is hers.

1 'You boggle shrewdly'

To 'boggle' literally means 'to shy like a startled horse'. It seems
appropriate for describing Bertram's reaction to the mess he has got
himself into because he constantly moves from lie to lie. Work out the
meaning of the King's next four words, 'every feather starts you'.

2 'An honourable gentleman'? (in pairs)

Parolles claims that Bertram is an 'honourable gentleman' (lines
236–7), and that he is as charming as other gentlemen. Remember,
Lavatch also had a fairly low opinion of the gentlemen at court. Talk
about whether you would use this concept of a 'gentleman' in a
production of *All's Well* for which you were responsible, and if so,
how would you show it?

3 Roving reporter (in small groups)

One member of the group is the reporter. The rest play the other
characters present during this scene (except for Bertram). The
reporter asks them for their opinions of Bertram at this point in the
action. Don't be afraid to ask searching questions about the character's motives and actions earlier in the play. For example: 'Captain
Dumaine, you have been criticising Lord Bertram's actions here, but
just how much truth was there in Master Parolles' stories about your
conduct in Paris?'

Or you could write this as an imaginary dialogue between a
reporter and several of the characters.

starts startles
just proceeding truthful evidence
Tricks charms
equivocal companion lying rogue
drum drummer
naughty orator worthless speaker

Satan . . . Limbo . . . furies
  Parolles compares the sexual
  desires of Bertram to the pains of
  hell and purgatory
credit confidence
motions activities
too fine hair-splitting

DIANA And this was it I gave him, being abed.

KING The story then goes false, you threw it him
      Out of a casement.

DIANA   I have spoke the truth.   *Enter* PAROLLES

BERTRAM My lord, I do confess the ring was hers.

KING You boggle shrewdly, every feather starts you.   230
      Is this the man you speak of?

DIANA   Ay, my lord.

KING Tell me, sirrah – but tell me true, I charge you,
      Not fearing the displeasure of your master,
      Which on your just proceeding I'll keep off –
      By him and by this woman here what know you?   235

PAROLLES So please your majesty, my master hath been an honourable
gentleman. Tricks he hath had in him, which gentlemen have.

KING Come, come, to th'purpose. Did he love this woman?

PAROLLES Faith, sir, he did love her, but how?

KING How, I pray you?   240

PAROLLES He did love her, sir, as a gentleman loves a woman.

KING How is that?

PAROLLES He loved her, sir, and loved her not.

KING As thou art a knave, and no knave. What an equivocal companion
is this!   245

PAROLLES I am a poor man, and at your majesty's command.

LAFEW He's a good drum, my lord, but a naughty orator.

DIANA Do you know he promised me marriage?

PAROLLES Faith, I know more than I'll speak.

KING But wilt thou not speak all thou know'st?   250

PAROLLES Yes, so please your majesty. I did go between them as I said,
but more than that, he loved her, for indeed he was mad for her,
and talked of Satan and of Limbo and of furies, and I know not
what. Yet I was in that credit with them at that time that I knew
of their going to bed, and of other motions, as promising her   255
marriage, and things which would derive me ill will to speak of;
therefore I will not speak what I know.

KING Thou hast spoken all already, unless thou canst say they are
married. But thou art too fine in thy evidence, therefore stand aside.
      This ring you say was yours?

DIANA   Ay, my good lord.   260

KING Where did you buy it? Or who gave it you?

DIANA It was not given me, nor I did not buy it.

Lafew and the King begin to doubt Diana's honesty. The King decides to arrest her for lying. She sends her mother to get help. Diana's final riddle makes it clear that Helena is pregnant.

Choose a line from the script opposite which makes a fitting caption for this picture.

1 'With child'

If you were designing a production, would you want Helena to appear visibly pregnant? According to Diana (line 291), she is more than twenty weeks pregnant, but this need not necessarily show.

common customer/strumpet
 prostitute
owes owns
surety bail

abused insulted
quit acquit
quick alive

KING Who lent it you?
DIANA   It was not lent me neither.
KING Where did you find it then?
DIANA   I found it not.
KING If it were yours by none of all these ways,   265
            How could you give it him?
DIANA   I never gave it him.
LAFEW This woman's an easy glove, my lord, she goes off and on at
      pleasure.
KING This ring was mine, I gave it his first wife.
DIANA It might be yours or hers for aught I know.   270
KING Take her away, I do not like her now,
            To prison with her; and away with him.
            Unless thou tell'st me where thou hadst this ring,
            Thou diest within this hour.
DIANA   I'll never tell you.
KING Take her away.
DIANA   I'll put in bail, my liege.   275
KING I think thee now some common customer.
DIANA By Jove, if ever I knew man, 'twas you.
KING Wherefore hast thou accused him all this while?
DIANA Because he's guilty, and he is not guilty.
            He knows I am no maid, and he'll swear to't;   280
            I'll swear I am a maid, and he knows not.
            Great king, I am no strumpet, by my life;
            I am either maid, or else this old man's wife.
                    [Pointing to Lafew]
KING She does abuse our ears. To prison with her!
DIANA Good mother, fetch my bail.   [Exit Widow]
                    Stay, royal sir.   285
            The jeweller that owes the ring is sent for,
            And he shall surety me. But for this lord,
            Who hath abused me, as he knows himself,
            Though yet he never harmed me, here I quit him.
            He knows himself my bed he hath defiled,   290
            And at that time he got his wife with child.
            Dead though she be, she feels her young one kick.
            So there's my riddle: one that's dead is quick –
            And now behold the meaning.

                    Enter HELENA and WIDOW

171

Helena enters and tells Bertram that she has fulfilled both his conditions. He promises to love her eternally. The King offers to find Diana a husband, and speaks the epilogue to the audience.

1 'Here's your letter' (in pairs)

In the 1992 production at Stratford, Helena took out a crumpled letter and began to read it aloud very slowly. She looked as if she was going to read out more of the cruel things in the letter, but very carefully tore it up on 'etc.' (line 303). It was a very moving moment. Talk about your own ideas for this line. Do you think that it should be presented as emotional and happy, or is Helena perhaps demanding her rights? List other possible interpretations for this moment, and talk together about which seems most appropriate to you. Share your ideas with the rest of the class.

2 'If . . .' (in groups of eight to ten)

Talk together about line 306. Do you think that the 'If' in line 305 makes Bertram's pledge of love ambiguous? Advise the actor how to stress 'If'.

3 All's well that ends well?

Would you end your production as 'happy' (Bertram really loves Helena), or as 'uncertain' (Bertram's love is in doubt)? Prepare two tableaux to show each possible ending. Which do you prefer? Why?

4 'All is well ended'

Write an alternative epilogue to the play for a modern audience, using three rhyming couplets.

---

exorcist someone who banishes or calls up spirits
Beguiles deceives
fresh uncroppèd flower virgin
meet appropriately

The king's a beggar because he is requesting applause as an actor
suit plea or request
hearts gratitude

KING   Is there no exorcist

Beguiles the truer office of mine eyes?   295
Is't real that I see?

HELENA   No, my good lord,
'Tis but the shadow of a wife you see,
The name and not the thing.

BERTRAM   Both, both. O, pardon!

HELENA O my good lord, when I was like this maid,
I found you wondrous kind. There is your ring,   300
And look you, here's your letter. This it says:
'When from my finger you can get this ring,
And are by me with child, etc.' This is done.
Will you be mine now you are doubly won?

BERTRAM If she, my liege, can make me know this clearly,   305
I'll love her dearly, ever, ever dearly.

HELENA If it appear not plain and prove untrue,
Deadly divorce step between me and you!
O my dear mother, do I see you living?

LAFEW Mine eyes smell onions, I shall weep anon.   310
[To Parolles] Good Tom Drum, lend me a handkercher. So, I thank
thee; wait on me home, I'll make sport with thee. Let thy curtsies
alone, they are scurvy ones.

KING Let us from point to point this story know,
To make the even truth in pleasure flow.   315
[To Diana] If thou beest yet a fresh uncroppèd flower,
Choose thou thy husband, and I'll pay thy dower.
For I can guess that by thy honest aid
Thou kept'st a wife herself, thyself a maid.
Of that and all the progress, more and less,   320
Resolvedly more leisure shall express.
All yet seems well, and if it end so meet,
The bitter past, more welcome is the sweet.   *Flourish*

[EPILOGUE]

The king's a beggar, now the play is done;
All is well ended, if this suit be won,
That you express content; which we will pay,
With strife to please you, day exceeding day.
Ours be your patience then, and yours our parts;   5
Your gentle hands lend us, and take our hearts.
                                                     Exeunt

Looking back at the play
Activities for groups or individuals

1 Happy ever after?

Your opinion about the likelihood of Helena and Bertram being happy in the future depends on how you interpret their characters. Do you think that Bertram has matured, and his love and respect for Helena have grown? Or do you think that any man who can lie as much as Bertram has done will ever make a faithful husband? Do you think Helena's love has survived? Or has her desire for Bertram made him merely a goal to be achieved? Collect evidence from the script to support your own opinions. Find someone in the group who disagrees with you and argue your case. Take care that you listen to your partner's reasoning and answer with evidence.

2 What do you think of Bertram?

Opinions about Bertram range from sympathetic – Helena has chased him all over Europe and he didn't like her anyway – to the frankly unprintable!

Either: make a collection of 'soundbites' (opinions one or two sentences long) on Bertram and arrange them as a display. Use quotations from the script and from a survey of your class. (It is a good idea to present the quotations in a different colour from the class's views.)

Or: retell the story from Bertram's point of view.

3 Ending well for Diana?

Diana has travelled from her home, apparently with some hardship, to confirm Helena's story. What do you think she would tell Violenta about her experiences when she returned to Florence?

4 The King's dating agency

The King has offered to find a husband for Diana. You might think that his experiences with Helena and Bertram would have made him more cautious about pairing people off. Who do you think he will suggest as a suitable partner for Diana? Give reasons for your choice.

5 Human graph (in groups of six)

The fortunes of various characters fluctuate in Act 5 Scene 3. Take one speaking part each (the actor reading the Widow also plays the Gentleman and the Gentle Astringer). Stand in a straight line down the centre of your acting space. As you read through Scene 3, move forward if your character seems to be doing well, or backwards if you are in trouble of any kind. All the characters will need to move both ways, but probably none so far or so often as Bertram.

6 All's well that ends . . .

The epilogue is sometimes cut as being irrelevant to a modern audience. Some critics consider it is merely a conventional plea for applause. Other critics argue that there is much more to it than that because it refers to the major themes of the play: social class and playing a part. If you were keeping it, how would you use it? For example, the cast could freeze and the King come forward to speak it, or someone could come back on-stage after the rest of the cast has gone. Talk together about how you would want your audience to react to the epilogue.

7 Parolles' fortune?

Parolles must be slightly cleaner by the end of the play, or Lafew would not want to borrow his handkerchief! What do you think will happen to Parolles after the end of the play? Do you think Bertram will remember their old friendship and take him back into the Rossillion household? Or will Parolles maintain a foothold at court through Lafew? Or will the Dumaine brothers try to get some kind of revenge for what he said about them in Florence? Or will he give up being a soldier and open a bistro? Or what?

8 Monsieur Parolles – this is your life!

One person plays the presenter and questioner. Get Parolles to tell his version of the story of each episode, then introduce each of the other characters, who will tell the same episode from their point of view.

9 The unmasking of Bertram

Bertram's exposure as a liar in Act 5 is paralleled in some ways by the unmasking of Parolles in Act 4. Talk together about how these two scenes reflect and complement one another.

What's *All's Well That Ends Well* about?

There is no simple answer to the question 'What's *All's Well* about?'. It has often been described as a 'problem play' because its bitter nature and ironical questioning of values leave audiences and readers perplexed and uncertain. Two of Shakespeare's other plays are also acknowledged to be 'problem plays', namely *Troilus and Cressida* and *Measure for Measure*, which were written during the same period (see page 188). On the surface, *All's Well* appears to be a comedy (because of its humorous scenes and because love seems to triumph in the end), but Bertram's unpleasantness, and the ambivalent tone throughout the play set it apart from Shakespeare's other comedies. Why Helena should love a man who constantly behaves so badly towards her, and only grudgingly accepts her at the end, is just one of the play's many puzzling features.

Shakespeare's custom was to base his plays on someone else's stories and *All's Well* is no exception. The main plot, the story of Helena and Bertram, comes from the *Decameron*, a collection of witty tales by the fourteenth-century Italian poet and story-teller, Giovanni Boccaccio. Shakespeare probably read it in the English version published in 1575. This is how the English translator, William Painter, told the story of Giletta of Narbonne:

> Giletta, a Phisitions doughter of Narbon, healed the French King of a Fistula, for reward wherof she demaunded Beltramo Counte of Rossiglione to husband. The Counte being married against his will, for despite fled to Florence, and loved another. Giletta, his wife by pollicie founde means to lye with her husband, in place of his lover, and was begotten with childe of two sonnes: which knowen to her husband, he received her againe, and afterwards he lived in great honour and felicitie.

Shakespeare added other elements to this basic plot. The story of Parolles raises difficult questions about the nature of military honour. The introduction of Diana and the Widow to help Helena stresses the strengths of women. The King, the Countess and Lafew present the traditional values of an older generation, in contrast with the younger characters in the play. Lavatch contributes an ironic sexual and social commentary on all he sees and hears.

Themes are ideas or concepts of fundamental importance which recur through a play, linking plot, character and language. Themes echo, reinforce and comment upon each other and upon the play as a whole. An important theme is declared in the first two lines of *All's Well* – birth and death. Bertram's old attitudes must die, and a new Bertram be delivered before he can finally become a genuine husband for Helena. Other characters can also be seen to experience some kind of rebirth or self-knowledge by the end of the play. Other themes include:

Loyalty 'will you undertake to betray the Florentine?'
(Act 4 Scene 3, lines 246–7).

Honour 'My honour's at the stake' (Act 2 Scene 3, line 141).

Women versus men 'Beware of them, Diana' (Act 3 Scene 5, line 14).

Age and youth 'the snuff/Of younger spirits'
(Act 1 Scene 2, lines 59–60).

Suffering and happiness 'The bitter past, more welcome is the sweet'
(Act 5 Scene 3, line 323).

Marriage 'Your marriage comes by destiny' (Act 1 Scene 3, line 48).

War 'O, 'tis brave wars!' (Act 2 Scene 1, line 25).

Faith and magic 'They say miracles are past' (Act 2 Scene 3, line 1).

Self-knowledge [Parolles] 'Who knows himself a braggart'
(Act 4 Scene 3, line 281).

Activities

a Write the story of *All's Well* as a mini-saga (in 100 words).

b Choose one theme from the list above and design a poster for the play, based on that theme.

c Explore the motives of Helena and Bertram in one of the following ways:
- 'Hot seating.' One member of the group takes on a role and is questioned by the others. (For example: 'Bertram, why did you call Diana "a common gamester"?' or 'Helena, why did you confront Bertram with Diana, rather than appearing immediately yourself?')
- 'Now tell me about yourself'. One person takes the role of either Bertram or Helena. The other acts as a psychiatrist.
- 'I understand.' Acting/writing as either Helena or Bertram, pour out your troubles to a sympathetic friend.

Helena – an actors' and critics' forum

There has been huge disagreement about Helena's personality and moral worth. These are some of the very varied opinions of her. They have been written or spoken by critics or actors over the past 200 years.

Helena is Shakespeare's loveliest creation.

There never was, perhaps, a more beautiful picture of a woman's love, cherished in secret, not self-consuming, but in silent languishment, not pining in thought, not passive and desponding over its idol, but patient, hopeful, strong in its own intensity and sustained by its own fond faith! Though poor and lowly, she shows true breeding and delicacy of feeling.

Bertram is brow-beaten by the King into marrying a girl he does not want. In a fairy-tale, Helena's motives would not be examined – of course the goose-girl wants to marry the prince. But she claims her reward in the face of Bertram's horrified recoil. This is realism. The kind of girl who engineers a marriage for herself is not the kind to worry about whether her bridegroom loves her or not; once the ring is on her finger, she feels there will be plenty of time to bring him round to her point of view.

In my salad days I accepted the view that Bertram was a loathsome mixture of snob and cad, whose treatment of the lovely and virtuous Helena was truly contemptible. I hold it still, but I have come to realise that he is in some ways sinned against as well as sinning, and that Helena, in spite of having many beautiful and pathetic things to say, is really an obnoxious young woman who merits, if ever a woman did, the classic title, 'designing minx'. For years I have mistrusted her, but it was only when reading the play with this lecture in mind that I realised how thoroughly she is on the make from start to finish, and how very well able she is to look after her own interests. She is the centre and focus of all medical interest in the play; she is the perfectly drawn presentation of the unqualified medical practitioner – the quack. I may be wrong, but I don't think Shakespeare's truly 'loveliest creation' would have opened a discussion on the keeping and losing of virginity with such a half-bred bit of riff-raff like Parolles.

She belongs to the 'doormat' type. They bear any amount of humiliation from the men they love, seem almost to enjoy being maltreated and ignored by them. They hunt them down in the most undignified way when they are trying to escape. The fraud with which Helena captures Bertram when he has left his home and country to get away from her, is really despicable.

Helena is a redeemer, a woman whose faith and integrity were going to save Bertram from his callowness.

Helena is a self-possessed young woman for whom the end always justifies the means.

Helena is the woman of the future for the actress of the future.

Two views from actors who have played Helena in Royal Shakespeare Company productions:

Far from being a kind of devouring tiger-female, she's desperately tentative. She is indeed manipulative, but then Fate keeps encouraging her, telling her she's right. She's an opportunist whose opportunities are made by the gods. But she's always diffident. Again, that Helena, the one who's chancing her arm, is in the script. And she, too, is humbled.

Harriet Walter, 1981

She's a very spiritual creature – she's led by determination and the power of will. It is such a shock to her when Bertram refuses her, and she finds herself in an excruciating position when he is forced to marry her; she even says she'll be his servant. When she gets that letter, she realises that he could die because of what she's done – that it's *her* fault. She leaves so that he can come back, and I think she is genuinely surprised when he turns up where she is. I don't believe it's prejudged; it happens on the moment, in the same way that her power is something outside her. There's a mixture between her power as a spiritual practitioner and her determination. Her love is complete and she will do anything for him – and she does. When she comes on at the end, Bertram is a broken man, and she redeems him. I feel they have a fighting chance of happiness.

Sophie Thompson, 1992

Activity

Create your own critics' forum to debate which of these views of Helena you feel is the most appropriate.

Social class, gender, age and power

Social class

Bertram does not want to marry Helena because she is not from the same social class as him:

> She had her breeding at my father's charge –
> A poor physician's daughter my wife? Disdain
> Rather corrupt me ever!
>
> Act 2 Scene 3, lines 106–8

In contrast, the King, though above both Bertram and Helena in social status, recognises that the true value of a person comes from personal worth, not title,

> Good alone
> Is good, without a name;
>
> Act 2 Scene 3, lines 120–1

Many Elizabethans, particularly those of high social standing, believed in a 'Chain of Being'. This was the belief that every creature and object in the universe occupied a fixed position in relation to everything else. Heaven was superior to Earth, and below God came the angels. On Earth, human beings were at the top of the Chain, above all the other creatures. The Chain progressed down through animals and plants to inanimate matter, such as water and gold. Within each species or class, everything had its place. For example, the rose was held to be supreme among the flowers, just as the monarch was thought to be the highest of all human beings. Ulysses' speech in *Troilus and Cressida* (Act 1 Scene 3, lines 75–137) can be read as a detailed defence of this theory of hierarchical status.

The ideology of the Chain of Being appealed greatly to people who occupied high social positions, because it justified their status and privilege. It is, of course, a highly questionable doctrine. By no means all Elizabethans believed it, and the absurdity of it is clearly shown in the claim that men are 'naturally' of higher status than women. In *All's Well* the King challenges the hierarchical assumptions of the Chain of Being in his suggestion that personal worth is more important than noble birth. But even he cannot break free from its basic assumptions, as he offers to grant Helena a 'title' to make her acceptable to Bertram.

Gender

In Shakespeare's day, Helena would have been seen as an unusual woman because she takes control of her own life. But she does not conform to the same pattern as similar women in other plays by Shakespeare. In several plays, women dress as men to try to achieve freedom. For example, Viola in *Twelfth Night* and Rosalind in *As You Like It* have to adopt a masculine appearance to achieve any kind of power over their lives. Women who defy the traditional codes of behaviour frequently destroy themselves in their search for power, such as Lady Macbeth in *Macbeth* or Goneril and Regan in *King Lear*.

a Identify the stages by which Helena takes an active part in deciding her own destiny. Make a list of the decisions she takes and the actions she performs as the play progresses.

b In many societies it is considered admirable for a man to be ambitious and tenacious. Talk together about words which could be used to describe a woman who displays the same qualities.

c Act out the parting of Helena and Bertram in Act 2 Scene 5, lines 47–86 ('Here comes my clog ... for our flight'). But, if possible, cast someone male as Helena, and female as Bertram. How does this gender change make you feel about Bertram's treatment of Helena?

Age and power

a Divide into five groups and work on one act each. Find all the references to Bertram's youth. Pool all your references, and talk about whether you feel sympathetic towards him because of his youth. Then debate whether you sometimes feel powerless, just because you are young.

b All kinds of things give power to the characters in *All's Well* (and in life itself!): experience, money, social position, background, military prowess, confidence, faith, and a host of other factors. Turn to the list of characters on page 1. Give a 'power score' from 1–10 for each character for each act. Decide what gives them the power they possess, and list these sources of power in order of importance.

The language of
All's Well That Ends Well

1 What is honour?

The words 'honour' or 'honourable' occur over forty times in *All's Well*. What do they mean to the people who use them? Research the uses of 'honour' in: Act 2 Scene 3; Act 3 Scenes 5 and 6; Act 4 Scene 2; Act 5 Scene 3. Copy and complete the table below to show what 'honour' means to each character. Which characters interpret 'honour' in more than one way? Identify the differences which social class and/or gender make.

Character	Scene	Quotation	Meaning
Bertram	2.3. 161	'dole of honour'	title
	3.6. 50	'instrument of honour'	good name
	4.2. 42	'honour 'longing to our house'	rich symbol
	4.2. 52	'mine honour . . . be thine'	reputation
Diana	4.2. 45	'mine honour'	chastity

2 Imagery

Imagery is the use of language to conjure up emotionally charged pictures in the mind. When the King says his honour is 'at the stake', the mental picture is of a bear tied to a post being attacked by dogs. It is a strong image to describe how the King feels about his situation. Identify the different image patterns which occur throughout *All's Well* (for example: war, flowers, falconry). Divide into five groups, take an act each, and list the images under your agreed headings. Present your findings as a wall display.

3 Typical language

In Act 2 Scene 5, Lafew says of Parolles: 'the soul of this man is his clothes': perhaps 'speech' could be substituted for 'clothes'.

Take your favourite (or most disliked) character from *All's Well*. Work through the script and make a list of quotations which typify your character's way of speaking. As a starting point, look to see if certain phrases or images crop up frequently.

4 Contrast and balance

Shakespeare enjoys playing with contrasting uses of words and rhythms. In the first few lines of Act 1 Scene 1 there are the following antitheses (contrasts):

delivering *v* bury
lack *v* abundance
immortal *v* death
living *v* death
admiringly *v* mourningly

The play's title seems to suggest a happy ending. The contradictions listed above perhaps give warning that all will not necessarily be well. Reread the final scene of the play closely, starting at line 278. List all the antitheses you find. Talk together about what Shakespeare's use of them here suggests to you about the mood of the play's ending.

5 Verse and prose

In Shakespeare's time, certain conventions existed about when to use verse or prose in a play. For example, servants would usually speak in prose, and the upper classes in verse. But Shakespeare was never afraid to break convention when it suited him. In *All's Well*, he frequently switches between verse and prose. Read Act 1 Scene 1 and Act 2 Scenes 4 and 5. Decide why the switches between prose and verse occur. The changes may be due to the social class of the speaker; to the mood of the speaker; to whether what is being said is comic or serious, or to point up the difference between the fairy-tale and the naturalistic elements of the play or . . .

6 Blank verse

Blank (unrhymed) verse was a very popular form in Shakespeare's time. Each line has five alternating unstressed (/) and stressed (X) syllables (iambic pentameter). For example, the King's final line before the epilogue:

/　X　/　X　　/　　X　/　X　/　X
The bitter past, more welcome is the sweet.

Try beating out the rhythm on the floor or table to help you.

Choose a verse passage of about ten lines and practise reading it in different ways to experience the underlying rhythm.

An actor's approach to
All's Well That Ends Well

1 Question and answer

This activity is a good way of opening a practical session. It also improves your knowledge of the play. You need enough pieces of card for the number of people in the class. Divide into five groups and take one act each. Go through your act and find quotations which consist of questions and answers. Write the questions and the answers on separate cards. Mix the cards up and place them face down on a table. Each person takes a card. Find your partner by just speaking the words on the card.

2 Auditioning

Choose a role which you would like to play. Select a speech which you think is a key one for the role. Learn the speech: audition for the role.

3 Bare bones (in small groups)

Reduce a whole scene to a series of single lines. Your aim is to tell the whole story of the scene using only the words of the play, but as economically as possible. Because you have to be so selective when doing this activity, it can be very illuminating to see how another group presents the same scene as your own. How do they justify their different choices of lines?

4 Mime

Tell the story of *All's Well* in a dumb show. This is one time when it is acceptable to overact! Remember to focus on the essential emotions and actions. Add music and sound effects if you have time.

5 Character groups (in small groups)

Select about ten quotations which you feel demonstrate the essence of a character of your choice. The words chosen may be either spoken by or about the character. Use these quotations to make a presentation to the rest of the class. Make your presentation as dramatic as possible (such as through choral speaking, exaggerated gestures, from different parts of the room, and so on).

6 Another soliloquy?

Write a soliloquy that Shakespeare left out. Choose a time when you feel that a character has something to say, but doesn't speak. For example: Helena immediately after the King has forced Bertram to marry her, or Diana when she finds out who Helena is, or Bertram after he has been promoted in Florence. Test the quality of your invented soliloquy by speaking it during a performance of the scene.

7 Dreams or nightmares?

Imagine that either Helena or Bertram has a dream just before the last scene. Act out the dream as dramatically as possible, using the other characters as accusing voices. If you have access to lighting and sound equipment, make it even more dramatically effective.

8 The status game (in groups of ten to twelve)

In *All's Well*, social standing is extremely important because status conveys power.

a One person acts as director and lines up the cast according to their status in Act 1. Where are the women? Does age confer status? Now change positions to show status at the end of the play. Who has had to move? Let the actor playing Bertram rearrange the order, then Lavatch, then one of the Dumaine brothers.

b Imagine that you are staging the play. Talk together about the ways in which you would exploit the subtle changes in status of the characters during the play and the complexity of relationships between different social classes in your production.

9 Character interpretation

Choose a short passage from the script in which only two people are talking. Try as many different ways of delivering their dialogue as possible, for example: seated, standing, close together, far apart, with and without eye contact, angrily, thoughtfully, compassionately, sneeringly, and so on.

10 Biographies

You are the biographer of Bertram, Helena and Parolles. Describe the early experiences which have shaped their characters.

Staging your production

In *All's Well*, the scenes shift rapidly from Rossillion to Paris and back again, to Florence and to the battlefield, to Marseilles and back to Rossillion. A production needs a very carefully designed set which can be adapted to suit all of these locations. Otherwise, the scene-shifters will spend more time on-stage than the actors!

Choosing the location and historical time in which to set the play is very important, because the appearance of the set can strongly influence the interpretation of the action. The director and the designer usually work together to design a set which will help the audience to understand the key issues of the play.

a *Either*: imagine that you have been given the task of designing a production. You have an unlimited budget and can choose your theatre space. Decide whether you would use a stage or an in-the-round production. Then talk together about what you would want to emphasise visually about *All's Well*. Would it be war, or fashion, or the power of the King or . . . ? Sketch your ideas for the set and costumes. (Books of historical fashions can be helpful.)

   Or: imagine that you have been asked to design for a struggling new professional company with cash-flow problems and no stage. The company is going to tour, giving performances in schools and sports centres. How inventive can you be?

   Then: whichever option you have chosen, justify your ideas and design an appropriate programme for the production.

b Imagine you are putting on a production of the play and want it to convey a particular message. For example, you could make your production strongly feminist, the triumph of a determined woman against seemingly impossible odds (or impossible men!). You could highlight the court scenes or the war scenes, to emphasise other 'readings' of the play. You could even present the play as a magical fairy-tale, with a conventional happy ending. As with any Shakespeare play many approaches are possible. Choose your 'reading' and explain how you would present it in your production.

Talk together about what you think
was in the mind of each of the
designers of the sets pictured here.

William Shakespeare 1564–1616

1564 Born Stratford-upon-Avon, eldest son of John and Mary Shakespeare.

1582 Marries Anne Hathaway of Shottery, near Stratford.

1583 Daughter, Susanna, born.

1585 Twins, son and daughter, Hamnet and Judith, born.

1592 First mention of Shakespeare in London. Robert Greene, another playwright, describes Shakespeare as 'an upstart crow beautified with our feathers . . .'. Greene seems to have been jealous of Shakespeare. He mocked Shakespeare's name, calling him 'the only Shake-scene in the country' (presumably because Shakespeare was writing successful plays).

1595 A shareholder in 'The Lord Chamberlain's Men', an acting company that becomes extremely popular.

1596 Son Hamnet dies, aged eleven.
Father, John, granted arms (acknowledged as a gentleman).

1597 Buys New Place, the grandest house in Stratford.

1598 Acts in Ben Jonson's *Every Man in His Humour*.

1599 Globe Theatre opens on Bankside. Performances in the open air.

1601 Father, John, dies.

1603 James I grants Shakespeare's company a royal patent: 'The Lord Chamberlain's Men' become 'The King's Men' and play about twelve performances each year at court.

1607 Daughter, Susanna, marries Dr John Hall.

1608 Mother, Mary, dies.

1609 'The King's Men' begin performing indoors at Blackfriars Theatre.

1610 Probably returns from London to live in Stratford.

1616 Daughter, Judith, marries Thomas Quiney.
Dies. Buried in Holy Trinity Church, Stratford-upon-Avon.

The plays and poems

(no one knows exactly when he wrote each play)

1589–1595 *The Two Gentlemen of Verona, The Taming of the Shrew, First, Second and Third Parts of King Henry VI, Titus Andronicus, King Richard III, The Comedy of Errors, Love's Labour's Lost, A Midsummer Night's Dream, Romeo and Juliet, King Richard II* (and the long poems *Venus and Adonis* and *The Rape of Lucrece*).

1596–1599 *King John, The Merchant of Venice, First and Second Parts of King Henry IV, The Merry Wives of Windsor, Much Ado About Nothing, King Henry V, Julius Caesar* (and probably the *Sonnets*).

1600–1605 *As You Like It, Hamlet, Twelfth Night, Troilus and Cressida, Measure for Measure, Othello, All's Well That Ends Well, Timon of Athens, King Lear.*

1606–1611 *Macbeth, Antony and Cleopatra, Pericles, Coriolanus, The Winter's Tale, Cymbeline, The Tempest.*

1613 *King Henry VIII, The Two Noble Kinsmen* (both probably with John Fletcher).

1623 Shakespeare's plays published as a collection (now called the First Folio).